# Hummingbird Sleep

EST. 75 1938
YEARS

THE UNIVERSITY OF GEORGIA PRESS 2013

# Hummingbird

THE UNIVERSITY OF GEORGIA PRESS

# Sleep

POEMS, 2009–2011

Coleman Barks

ATHENS AND LONDON

Published by The University of Georgia Press
Athens, Georgia 30602
www.ugapress.org
© 2013 by Coleman Barks
All rights reserved
Designed by Kaelin Chappell Broaddus
Set in 10/15 Quadraat by Kaelin Chappell Broaddus

Most University of Georgia Press titles are
available from popular e-book vendors.

Printed digitally

Library of Congress Cataloging-in-Publication Data
Barks, Coleman.
Hummingbird sleep : poems, 2009–2011 / Coleman Barks.
118 p. ; 23 cm.
Includes bibliographical references.
ISBN 978-0-8203-4504-8 (pbk. : alk. paper) —
ISBN 0-8203-4504-0 (pbk. : alk. paper)
I. Title.
PS3552.A6717H86 2013
811'.54—dc23

2012029628

British Library Cataloging-in-Publication Data available

For Lisa Starr

and

the grandchildren:

    Briny—born July 17, 1991

    Tucker—born August 9, 1998

    Keller—born October 10, 1998

    Woody—born July 15, 2001

    Henry—born August 7, 2012

And all the possibilities.

# CONTENTS

Hummingbird Sleep

## Starting Out from Ted Hughes' Letters

He would have his children make lists of similes
and reward them thruppence each for the good ones.
So & so is like so & so.

This list rose up in me when I read that.
A pot is like a possibility.
A beef stew is like a pile of leaves with children hiding in it.
The end of a love affair is like the rest of my life.
A pair of glasses set out on the desk is like forgetting your name.
A rainy late afternoon playing the board game SORRY!
with two grandsons, Tuck (11) and Woody (7),
and my son Benjamin (45) is like
the peach basket James Naismith nailed ten feet up
above the YMCA door as he was inventing the sport of basketball
at Springfield College in Massachusetts, December 1891,
trying to keep his delinquent students active but noncombatant,
indoors during the winter. They used a soccer ball.
I would love to see it happen, to honor Dr. Naismith's ingenuity,
that every NBA team should play one quarter a month
with a soccer ball. It would put some Globetrotter
slapstick into the passing and courtlong hailGoose shots.

The joy of being side by side touching shoulders with someone
so loved and different from one's own self is like a simile.
Being wonderfully full of oneself is like
feeling mean and forgetting your heart.
Surely something will survive this
self-destructing love that pulls us along.

Gregory of Nyssa says there is a sort of watchful sleep
where one is neither awake nor not-awake,
not caught in either opposite but fusing both
in a place where mind has gone out of itself
but is not yet under the control of what

we might call a creative imagination,
a giving-in to some sovereign, wider intelligence,
the source of simile and metaphor, say.

Gregory of Nyssa writing subtle comments
in whatever language he did in the wilds of fourth-century Cappadocia,
on whatever surface he wrote on with whatever he wrote with,
his notes on the nature of awareness as it floats
between more nameable conditions, is like
driving a car and talking into the rearview mirror,
to someone in a far-off bed, as one does with the new OnStar technology.

You touch the mirror in a certain place, the bottom left,
to hang up, or it is like Thoreau's concept of economy,
what he went out to Walden Pond to explore.
He wanted to be careful how he spent the spirit's energy,
his vitality. Like me talking about that,
one April Thursday in 1981 to a class of sleepy sophomores
who rouse to the idea only when I confess
that I never buy shaving cream but rather collect those elusive bits
of handsoap from all around the house and save them in a cup
and stir that with a cheap shaving brush for lather.

Then I ask them their secrets for saving a bit here, bit there.
What I mostly get are ways of ripping off vending machines.
Warm water poured in the coin slot, the two quarters on a string trick,
and a very elaborate bill-folding scotchtape caper.

And never pay the toll road tolls, just make a gesture of throwing
and drive through leaving them whirring, clanging and flashing in your wake.
Nobody ever comes after you, or if they do, say the change
is on the ground back there, and there always is some.

Where are these clever petty-cash schemes leading,
and what are they like? Like something decided-on,
a cleared-off campsite on the forest floor,
a starting-out place, and Plotinus.

Because that master said in Greek in the bright sun of Alexandria,
or maybe Rome, *playing*. The power of growth
in plants, in the ground itself, and surely in us,
is a form of *play*, all motion, even the movement of this sentence,
leads us playfully toward contemplation,
those quadrants of sky the soul aspires to.

And what is this *contemplation*
Plotinus says we are all in the midst of becoming?
Inner opening into emptiness,
where everything and nothing are no longer *alike*,
but boundaryless play inside a single point, the one,
where I have gotten enough sleep,
where I feel calm and ready behind-my-eyes,
settled and potentially hilarious in nervous system and brain,
waiting for the beckoning cabin-call of how we *begin*
to watch a movie, or read a novel, or listen to new music.

In the frontyard lives the oldest thing around, a white oak
that I used to say is my love for the world,
that I now would just call love as it is,
belonging to nobody, no metaphor, the very.

## My Face and My Voice

Tenderhearted people sometimes misunderstand each other,
not that I am always good in that way,
but on the night in question, I feel like I was.

My face can look angry when I am not,
and me not know it.

I have received a letter that reminds me of this.
I should be more careful of my affect, how I present myself.

The Buddhists and the Taoists talk about *the original face*,
your mystical, essential identity that will outlast the universe.
Would I prefer to show that to the world?
I would. I think I would,
but I don't really know what I'm asking for.

No name, no return address,
just Boise ID 817_ _.


Mr. Barks,

I have been thinking about writing this letter for almost a year. I would like to write it and release the feelings I have and move on.

You came to speak at Boise State University last fall. I was so excited to finally be able to see you in person as I have been a fan of yours (through NPR) for years. I have always loved your deep voice, and when it is matched with Rumi's poetry, it is magic.

Your poetry reading was wonderful. My friend and I enjoyed it very much. After the reading we stood in line for well over an hour to get our books signed. I brought with me my hardback copy of *The Soul of Rumi*. I was excited to be able to have your signature on it.

By the time we got to you (and had waited so long), I am sure you were tired. When you went to sign my book, you asked my name and went through the motions of signing. I don't care that you didn't want to talk to me—you had been talking to people all night—but the look on your face I did care about. You had such an angry look on your face when you handed the book back, all I could do was imagine that I reminded you of someone you really disliked.

I remember going home that night and telling my husband how cold and angry you seemed. He knew how disappointed I was. I have put my Coleman Barks Rumi books away. I don't read any of them anymore. My point of this letter is not to be mean or angry toward you. I just want you to realize that you are a celebrity in your world and the people you meet are there to thank you for what you do. Please be more careful how you treat your fans.

I appreciate the time you have taken to read this.


So forgive me, nameless ex-reader, and anyone else
to whom I have let my unconscious anger flare
from inside this mask I call a face. My fear,
my jealousy, my stuckup strutting around.
I am sorry I disappointed you.

And please forgive me, everyone,
every time I have not been deeply enjoying
your presence, dear biped, triped, and no peds at all,
just a slick slow slide.
I forget how much I love snakes.

There is great mystery in the face,
the heart-mirror one sees into and through.
The woman looked in my face and saw something
contradictory to the words I had been saying
of Jelaluddin Rumi, my better, my teacher.
She saw darkness, and she is right.
I hope to clear this visage before I die,
though it probably won't change much now.

Some people thrive on facial expressions, unlike me and my beard-face
and the birds who have so little wrinkle-room on their beaks
but such complicated melodious voices.
Sing and smile, you fool, or the snakeline public will eat you.

Someday I will be in Boise again,
reading this poem with her in the audience listening.
Will she come forward? I think she will.
Toward the end of the signing line,
as the very end itself, to this.

You are a good writer. That letter is so clear
and brave and hurt and trying to be true it set me going,
woke me up a little. Thank you. Would you like to dance?

Though now I reconsider.
She is not going to ever come to anything I do,
unless she hears how I am out using her letter this way.
Is it legally mine or hers? She did not sign it
or put the little copyright "c" in a circle at the bottom,
which now I do.

Copyright. Coleman Barks

There is more to ask about the original face.
Is it an individual thing?

William Blake felt so strongly this aspect of identity.
He claims to *remember* works of art he created
before the ones he is working on in his current human form.

There is a letter he writes in September 1800,
moving a big load of books and prints to a new working location.
"Now begins a new life. We set out between six & seven in the morning of a
Thursday with sixteen heavy boxes and portfolios full of prints. All was cheer-
fulness and good humor on the road and yet we could not arrive at our cot-

tage before half past eleven at night owing to the necessary shifting of our luggage from one chaise to another for we had seven different chaises and as many different drivers."

I hear him yelling inside his laughter, *Slipping to the left again, Henry, the left. We must let Edward have more of the angels. He has need of them.*

"In my brain are studies and chambers filled with books and pictures of old which I wrote and painted in ages of eternity before my mortal life and those works are the delight and study of archangels. Why, then, should I be anxious about the riches and fame" of London, Paris, the scenes he calls *mortality.*

"Felpham is a sweet place for study because it is more spiritual than London. Heaven opens here on all sides her golden gates. My wife and sister both are well, courting Neptune for an embrace."

Surely he means they were at the beach, *courting Neptune for an embrace,* in water somewhere, a bath or a pond. In our best bouyancy, we do want to be held by ocean.

I have had a dream where I am watching a book being set page by page, a book of *Blake's Prose.* There are fish ornaments in the lefthand corners and boxes on the top righthand with the faces of Chinese patriarchs, carefully carved features, beards and eyes, wildly nourishing to what Blake calls Poetic Genius, the making part, whatever it is in us that intends truth and recognizes beauty, and loves, adapting to each weakness uniquely, to *make* something intricate.

Blake loves books and image making about as much as a human being can love anything.

They are life-giving for him, impregnating and birthing. I don't know that a book of *Blake's Prose* exists. Someone should compile the juicy parts from letters, the memoranda and marginal notes on other people's writing, dreams recorded in *The Marriage of Heaven and Hell,*

the prefatory note to *Jerusalem*.
Now the volume has been dreamed, it must appear.

More from the Original Face.
*Speaking:*

This face breaks open with compassion
for how the world is hurting.
Then with meditation Buddha repairs me,
gives me eleven small faces and one great one,
none of them either male or female, both and one.
Call me Kwan Yin.
Very useful for the work, those variable eleven faces.

*Now* will the faceless woman return to talk
with the friend of clear green water?
I do not think she shall.

I think she will. She's here.

We send feelings out foraging in the mail and the email,
not knowing what they will come back with.

The teaching spreads out over phenomena.
That is one way of it.

Another is it cannot be seen or said.
Covering everything, but tinier than lighted air.

Take care of yourself.

## Lightning Bugs and the Pleiades

They belong with this piece of land as much as I do.
I have lived here since 1968. They since . . . do we know?
Wonder what the Cherokee word for their flickering selves is,
and back beyond that, the shell-circle builders' word.
Five thousand years.

They were one of the first things—
the second after fall color, and third after twilight
April-gold—that I tried to write down
the beauty of and my love for,
at twelve years old.

So I come back around here at near the end,
to the same subject,
rather the same flying lights, different subject.

That first lightning bug poem was about
the disillusionment of wanting to collect,
to bottle up in a mason jar such fascinating beauty.

Every child knows the mess of that.
You catch thirty in a jar and take them home.
Then they stop going on and off. They glow up, stay on,
melt together, die, turn black, and smell bad.

You throw them out, a cliché for the consequences
of possessive desiring. Their beauty needs
to stay free to overwinter in the ground,
as does mine.

I have identified two young volunteer trees
growing in my yard as black locusts.
The hill I grew up on was called Locust Hill
because a grove of these grew on the side of it.

That was in the dell where we children
ran after lightning bugs, little poets looking
for the right word, letting them light
on the backs of our hands, then scintillate
off, which is all they do for the fourteen days
of their short lives, with surely some sleep.

They want and they want.
They look and flash and fly to mate,

trying to prolong the lineage that brought them here,
these spark-figurations sacred to Orpheus,
that somehow are related to orphans and doves,
and sisters to the rain-golden mist over the ocean
with the sun going down that we call the Pleiades.

People have looked up at night, and out, and down,
and told stories about stars and lightning bugs
in this vanishing of our longing and those lights.

Every life is incomplete,
with much left undone, half-done.

I mourn the paucity of lightning bugs
in the air of this earth-patch yard.
They have dwindled noticeably the last forty years.
Maybe in twenty more they will come back strong,
even more numerous than they were in the 1940s.

Maybe this is not part of the big dying-out going on,
of polar bears, frogs, rainforest,
red wolf and grey fox, but it probably is.

Nobody knows what to do.
We are waiting to be told.
Anything, we will try it,
even driving our cars less.

The alder tree is also sacred to Orpheus.
I love to write inside an overarching creeksound,
on the bank where the alder lives
with a black tupelo and a Carolina silverbells.

My grandson Woody
fell in love with a pine cone once in Yosemite.
By statute, you are not allowed to carry *anything* out of the park,
but no one, not even the ranger, could separate that young man
from the single pine cone almost as big as his head
he had chosen for his soul to feast upon.

They open, you know, as roses do, pine cones,
from being tightly wrapped in themselves
to being how we all might become
this very moment—pointy, sinewy,
and ready for the fire of someone else's presence.

## My Segment on the NewsHour

I misquoted the Bible on national television.
A preacher caught me, emailed, *Not Luke 17:12, Luke 17:21.*
The one and two got transposed in my apparatus.
I go back to have a look.

It truly is something, what Jesus says in answering the Pharisees,
about when the kingdom of God is coming.
He says it is not like that.
It will not *come with observation.*
You will not say, *Lo, here* or *Lo, there.*

Because it is not something
that is arriving in space and time,
not anything to be *observed.*

*For behold, the kingdom of God is within you.*

But that is just half the story.
The Gospel of Thomas has what I take to be the full text.

*The kingdom of God is within you*            Thomas, Saying 3
*and all around you.*

*Split a piece of wood. I am there.*            Saying 77
*Lift up a stone, and you will find me there.*

The holiest thing then, the *kingdom,* is inside,
the observing consciousness, the deep core of being,
and outside, the brown thrasher, the little girl skipping
over the squares of the sidewalk, the universe itself
that, so far as we know, is unlimited.

It would be best here to start singing and dancing
for the spacious joy of inside and outside.

Mary Oliver saw me give a reading once.
She asked afterward what was that
you were doing with your feet? I like that.
*A little buckdancing I fall into.*

## Accordion Sections

When I find a new poet that I love,
I mark poems in the table of contents
that I want to go back to and read to other people,
on the phone, or in the Clubhouse.

But this one I have marked every poem
as I read it. They are each so necessary
for the beauty of the world to be shown itself by
and made delicious with. Her first name is spelled Wislawa,
but the l has a crooked crossbar in the middle,
which I learn is pronounced as a w in Polish,
and the two w's as v's, so it's vis-WAH-vah,
last name, S-z-y-m borska, shim-BOR-ska.

She was born in 1923, July 2, somewhere in Poland.
Me in 1937, Tennessee. Why am I just now at seventy-one
learning about her whom I read with such urgency?

The note says she has worked as a poetry editor, columnist, translator.
My arms look old today, splotched and not like my arms.
They look like they are dying.
I will tell my doctor Sam Griffin that,
little old watchmaker with his eccentric glasses.
He takes them apart at the center when he talks to me.

On the back cover my friends, Ed Hirsch and Robert Hass,
say how wonderful she is, but they never told me.
This book has been out since 1998, twelve years.
I should actually read the Sunday New York Times literary section.

Lazy, I was a long time finding Cormac McCarthy too.
My friend Jim Kilgo kept saying, Coleman, you would love this guy
and he's from Knoxville, just upriver from you in Chatt-nooga.
O the lush riverrun bourbonic prose of Suttree, my favorite.

I was physically angry, as if Dante had never been told
there were troubadours next door, and Shakespeare
never hearing of Marlowe or Cervantes.
Was there a translation of the good Don he might have looked at?
Did Emily read Walt? A little bit, but not he her. He could not have,
unless he snuck in her bedroom while the family was out at a funeral,
opened the cedar chest, and undid one of the fascicles
its length of pink ribbon. Thought, What have we here, camerado?
*Exultation is the going of an inland soul . . . ,*
for a walk along the shore? *To sea, lad. Into the stuff.*

Keats left a note once on Wordsworth's mantel at Rydal Mount,
not finding him home, always out walking, the both of them,
different paths, no path. *We do adore the animal-creep.*

The *redemptive handrail* is her phrase
for not-knowing what poetry is.
She holds to that not-knowing handrail,
the blessed ignorance of what this is,
this walking around talking.

My son built me a handrail on the left side going down
the stairs so steep into my redclay basement,
where children and their children have built roads, the same roads,
for little cars and trucks, bridges over the impossible abyss
where we stand and watch them work their play.

This handrail is unique because it has a break in it,
hiatus for the fusebox door to open through.
I had not foreseen that that would have to be
when I decreed its leftness going down.
Truth be told, I like handrails on both sides.
The hiatic handrail keeps me alert.

Sufis have a joke about theology.
There are these fish, the theologians,

who like to school together in study groups
to consider the possible existence of the ocean,
the joke being they are swimming in it.
God is everywhere and everything, nothing but God,
what the zikr says. So they have ninety-nine names
for nothingness, the suchness of THAT,
with one other name never spoken.

God is so enormously vast and minute and pervasive
that he-she-it-we-you-they cannot be held in word or set of words,
so enjoy the swim-inside-mystery. Szymborska uses sky instead of sea.

CLOUDS

I'd have to be really quick
to describe clouds —
a split second's enough
for them to start being something else.

Their trademark:
they don't repeat a single
shape, shade, pose, arrangement.

Unburdened by memory of any kind,
they float easily over the facts.

What on earth could they bear witness to?
They scatter whenever something happens.

Compared to clouds,
life rests on solid ground,
practically permanent, almost eternal.

Next to clouds
even a stone seems like a brother,
someone you can trust,
while they're just distant, flighty cousins.

Let people exist if they want,
and then die, one after another:
clouds simply do not care
what they are up to
down there.

And so their haughty fleet
cruises smoothly over your whole life
and mine, still incomplete.

They aren't obliged to vanish when we're gone.
They don't have to be seen while sailing on.


I will work my foamy-intricate, slow cloud-way
back to front from close to now to 1957 when she was thirty-four.

She says, "I prefer, where love is concerned, *nonspecific anniversaries*,
which can be celebrated every day."

My dream last night was majestic in its wisdom, I wake feeling that,
but all I can recall is this detail, that I was translating James Dickey's poems
into Spanish peanuts, the little round ones with purplish, papery integuments
wrapping each individually, those by the handful, translating his poems
into another language, which was those, Spanish peanuts, and bananas,
then a light yellow paste made of the two.
My work as translator is strange, but tasty.

Sufis are so elegantly innocent, like the Upanishads
saying *aham brahmaas mi*,
that outrageous distillation of human dignity,
*I am the divine. I am the ultimate.* That we do not know
who first said or who keeps saying it, before and apart
from any religion, because if you *are* the thing,
you do not need doctrine or sanctuary, or even a high place,
so you can keep playing in the basement,
as voices slipslide across each other like accordion sections.

What is a nonspecific anniversary?
Something happening again
but not anything in particular,
the passing of unmarked time,
like a really really long train,
with us watching at an intersection,
in a backedup line of cars,
and us on the train too, waving to ourselves,
cloudshape steady in the moving windows.

## Our Next Dying

The reading of the fossil record now
is that 250 million years ago there was a Great Dying.
99.9 percent of everything then living
died, which included some very odd-looking, snub-nosed,
four-legged mammals. From the few small lizards left,
the dinosaurs evolved and thrived for the next
200 million years. Then they were wiped out
along with much else, 45 million years ago.
Scientists have found the big crater in Antarctica
where the asteroid landed that caused the dustcloud
that precipitated the Great Dying. The Gulf of Mexico
is the hole they think the other one made
that eradicated the dinosaurs in the second killoff.
And now I hear that there may have been
three other dyings-out not caused
by gigantic rocks from space.

We human beings evolved from life forms left
after the second seven-mile-wide rock
struck the earth just south of New Orleans.
These are all scientific best-guesses.

A different guess is that along with human beings
evolved and traveled inside the various forms
a tremendously valuable quality that some people,
with infinite variations, call soul—the part
that recognizes beauty and feels the wonder
of ecstatic interconnectivity with all life.

Rumi did not know about the fossil record
that reveals the Great Dying and the Dinosaur Wipeout,
but his notion of the soul's growing does go back
past those events to our mineral beginnings 5 billion years ago.
Then through the quicker slowmotions of plant life and animal life,

on to this walking-erect biped who invents language, myth, art,
and all manner of geared, axled, and electron-flow technology.
On then to an unimaginable next stage, next and next.
He claims that the impulse to give in to our next dying
so that we can be radically transformed by it
is joyfully inherent in the process.

I want a technology that will let me go down inside
the molecules of this table where I am writing,
to glide through molecular structures into spaciousness.

I also want to travel out past galaxies and planets
and gaze down into black holes.
Such a technology would go there with just our seeing
and so without danger to these frail instruments of soul travel,
these bodies. A prop plane I was in once
circled my hometown on the night of the July 4 fireworks
just as the big stuff was lighting up. We were seeing
luminous jellyfish drifting toward the surface
to dissolve in tiny particles.
We could not hear a blessed thing.

My teacher Bawa Muhaiyaddeen
told me the cosmos is just a speck
and that the heart-center can go all over it
from one side of the universe to the other
in a millisecond, as fast as you can think it.

I have not yet got the knack
of his no-baggage, no-airport quick-flight,
but I do know this sort of soul travel,
the distance, and all the little towns,
the restaurants along the road, the barns,
the quarry lakes, that one travels
inside love for another human being.

From, *I did not know it was you,*.

On until, *I am so grateful for how we love each other*.

There is something I am not mentioning,
the mystery we move within,
something like a presence,
the ocean of *ilm*, the *qalb* of the heart.
I hide my ignorance and hide *from* my ignorance,
my inability to say what I feel,
with Arabic terminology for spirit-things.
*Ruh* is their word for soul.

And this rueful, dear life is so much more
than anyone can say, this we are and move through,
so like a glowing cloud, a hazelnut of live,
synchronicity-delighting music.

I am shown almost every day
how closely meshed those of us
who love each other are.
Truly all one thing
that can never be said.

I offer no proof
other than my whole life
and your whole life
as they dissolve in each other
as we read or speak,
as we watch or dance,
as we play or sing, as we walk
from being indoors
to being out.

## Word Choice

In 1961 Gary Snyder's Zen teacher
tells him when language comes quickly and easily,
it is more closely allied to one's internal state.

If you strain to find words,
or if you wait for them,
that pausing invalidates the words
when they do come,
makes them stopgap, second-third choices,
not living sentences.

I find some truth in this,
and some bullying of truth by spontaneity.

Consider a word like *meretricious*.
It hides back in the eighteenth century.
Someone who knew Latin made *meretricious* up.
He needed a word that meant falsely beautiful,
an attractiveness with the fake shine of money on it.
*Meretrix* is Latin for a high-end prostitute, call girl,
escort service companion for traveling executives.

People used to make up words more than they do now,
when they knew Latin and Greek better than we do.

I would like to ask Cormac McCarthy
how he came upon *marcessant*.
*Withering, but not yet fallen off.*

He uses it in *Suttree* to reveal
a very old woman's arms *marcessant* in the lamplight,
turning the pages of a family album.

In a couple hundred years *marcessant*
may reach to the status of *meretricious*.
Language is slow to move in such remote areas.

Mary Oliver uses *slubby*.
It comes from the Dutch, who know a lot about mud,
in their lowdown Brueghal-dance ways.

*Slubby* names the miry-slick stickiness
where ducks might love sliding into a lake.

I love another wet-earth word, *sillion*. Firmer,
the curve of a furrow the plow has just turned over,
used only one place in poetry as far as I know.
*Sheer plod makes plow down sillion shine.*

I shall now display more mud-related words.
*Mumbledypeg*, the knife game where the one who loses
has to dig the peg out with his teeth,
the peg that has been pounded deep with the heel of the knife,
and Barry Heywood goes after it with such earth-eating ferocity,
he comes up spewing soil from his dirt-face that has now a center
with between his teeth like an ivory narwhal horn, the peg.

A path through tall grass after heavy rain
feels *clodgy* underfoot. Earth sticking to a spade
when you are digging, that piece of ground
is *cledgy* to work with.

*Gawm* is especially sticky and foul-smelling mud.
A wagon axle could get gormed up with gawm.
*Gubber* is black anaerobic mud composed
of rotting organic material, no breath letout-tatall.

A *clod* is fairly coherent earthen wonderment.
A *paunch*, among other things, is what a cow does
with its hoof to a clod. It paunches about
crumbling the plowed field to mudproper.
Muddling through, there is a thick pudding
you call *stodge*. *Stug* is more watery.
Silt you already know, very fine.

People used to patch their houses with stug.
I have a place I stug.

What do you call the little ridges of parallel tunnels
that mud daubers make? Toy quonset dobberdoms.
I am become a scholar of mud.

Pug is a kind of loam, the tacky yellow sort.
A slough is a mudhole,
though it may have deep places and be connected to a river.

Smeery means a wet mud-surface, not clodgy or slobbed up.
Slob and slub, more thick-mud words.
Slub will take your shoe off and keep it.

With these mud-words you can trade vowels around,
because that is the world they are in.

He come home all of a slub.
He slubbed home through the stodge.

Sleech is river sediment used for manure.
Slurry, mud diluted to cream.

Spannel means to make the indoors like the out,
as a dog might, splushing in the slough,
then spanneling through the kitchen.

And since embodiment is the river's use of mud,
to scud the springflood with fleering mist is joy.

## Snow Day, the Word God, and the
## Threat of the Power Going Off

You know how I know
there is something for the word *God* to refer to?
So it is good to have that word I never use?
But this once. Is.

I live in the deep South, and it is snowing,
March 1, 2009, 4:30 in the afternoon,
my face looking up in it,
bigflake-slow, everywhere-snow,
four inches crunchy, four inches in the air,
so silent. There is more.

I just came back from the Waffle House.
Three eggs over medium, sausage, sliced tomatoes
instead of grits, dry wheat, coffee.
Lord, in comes Briny,
with three other high school senior girlfriends.

The beauty of Rachel has to try on my Afghan Cossack hat.
I throw it to her across the room.

I go to the store for candles,
expecting the power to go off later.
Four yellow Aloha Bay, wax made from palm oil.

All of this is my answer to the God question.
Parts of the whole, be still, you candle flames.

The little cedar trees in my yard are bowed down like Muslims
stuck in one prayer posture, toptips to the earth,
adoration complete.

I get a broom to bat them back into more livable positions.
They are eager to respond.

The slow loading of their arms begins again.
I'll come back in the morning.
I'll come back in the night
to do this again, such ecstatic baby-cedars, babysitter.

Snow day tomorrow, no school, Writers' Club already planned.
I can hardly stand it,
so I make a fire in the fireplace,
read a random chapter in Boswell's *Life of Johnson*,
and walk back out in it one more time before dark.
I will be seventy-two next month.

I know this makes little God-sense to my friends in Minnesota.
But we have not had snow like this in years.
Forecast is fifty degrees tomorrow.

Briny and her friends walked all the way across town
from Benjamin's house, everybody outdoors, equally wealthy.

Just here—I do swear it—the power blinks off,
back on, now off for good.

I shall finish this in the early nineteenth century,
burning palmwax, with candlelit, handwritten script.

I bend to light the chemical log that will light the red oak
and realize these are the maypop matches
Cole saw somewhere and bought me for Christmas,
maypop flower on the box, no writing,
long wooden matches like I love.

That is what I call deeply thoughtful.
And then there is Briny again, another day,
walking out to a restaurant with her boyfriend
in just sandals in the snow.
Benjamin is calling after her with shoes.
*I will learn my lesson,* she says.

I bow with the snowy cedars again
to touch the ground for that
and stay there touching the cold cold
as though stranded in some station of the beloved,
which I am.

## Old Men Out Walking

I have watched old men walk around this neighborhood
for over forty years. Now I am one of them,
or more than one.

Deliberate striders some, some swaggery with a stick,
swinging it at times in a two-handed baseball arc to the side,
pushing at gates with the extended tip,
signposts and telephone poles.

One of them talks into a tape recorder,
everything he remembers about the houses,
how they have been variously peopled,
graced and disgraced, porched and deporched.
He publishes those memories in a book
called *Strolls around Athens*. The blessed
Dean William Tate.

I stop to write notes to myself,
standing there near someone doing yardwork,
so I won't have to remember,
short-term fading fast.

There is a bench halfway where I sit and listen to birds,
in loving memory of, within living earshot,
three benches looking slanchwise, one at the other, the other.

People say, *Hey Coleman*, from cars.
I mostly cannot see through the reflection,
but I act like I know who, not fooling anyone.

Light rain sprinkles.

Ambience, *ambit*. Is that the area a king can walk easily around
in a day, his kingdom, his ambulatory ambition?
Kingdom getting smaller.

Then they break loose all boundary,
like Ed Hicks' father, taking off for the river
in the center of the swamp, a milkweed twilight float-tuft.

On Mt. Vernon a woman sits in her circular brick driveway
right down on the bricks picking at something
very tiny in the almost-dark.

Have you lost your mind?

*Yaaayuhh.*

That's good.
I'll be joining you soon.

Why do I keep going back to Plotinus?
What am I looking for?

Another sentence like, *To behold beauty is to become oneself beautiful.*

Or, *Because it has no size, the Soul's nature is sufficiently ample*
*to contain the whole cosmic body in one and the same grasp.*

Or, *the Soul is coterminous with its expression, and this expression*
*is of that grandeur intended by its form.*

I feel the truth of that.
Something like a grandeur
is trying to be expressed
by old men out walking, Plotinus, Meister Eckhart,
Chesterton, Mark Twain. Jelaluddin Rumi. Gary Snyder.
My father. I love these walking fathers.

It is good to be out in the eager air,
on the side of a certain hill,
or around a bottomland island.

Maybe we can yet walk together
and come close to saying the truth of whatever we know.

Plotinus might say, as we fall in with him,
that pretending to knowledge is a kind of play,
and play is good for approaching full contemplation,
where the soul can rest.

The Cherokee word for the center of the world
is *Ahyali-Ahlohee*. A name not just for that hill
but for the whole river valley, the island, the hills and mountains,
though most have individual names, *Chattanooga*
being the most magnificent, *rock-rising-to-a-point*.

I have no right to,
but I claim that my love for this air-ground-water,
wind, cloud, and all the plants,
and all the creatures living here, that have ever lived here,
lets me name it. *Yallalohee*, call then this place
we human types have chosen
for the last fifteen thousand years, and beyond,
the land-stretch between Missionary Ridge and Signal Mountain,
bounded by Raccoon and Lookout, with Moccasin Bend
at the center, stretching north unbound by any natural feature
to say, the White Oak Cemetery Duckpond,
where my parents are buried beneath a cedar tree.

*Yallalohee*, a musical shortening of the Cherokee
for the center of the earth, and all that gathers round the center
and radiates out from the remains of a silo
into a great wandering-rope circumference,
a walking place for old men and old women,
the young and the yet-to-be,
a winding umbilicus path, also *Yallalohee*.

We cast a circular net. We drag it in, slowly pulling unevenly
the circumference to its center. Let us become that,
a way crumpling into an origin.

Sometimes we catch a fish or a boot, turtle,
a piece of boatwood, never the water itself.
The beauty of mystery cannot be contained
in any thing or word.

This island, and all of Yallalohee,
have figured mightily in my dreams for decades,
as the site of a fabulous learning community,
one that has let go the net,
relaxing into some transcendence of the individual self.

I want to build or help build a path around
this island's outer edge, as close to the riverbank as possible,
with steps going down to the water every so often,
where you can look in and see what's cooking.

The walking will be the beginning of the learning
and the end. Stay on the delicious bank edge,
if that is your tendency, as it is often mine.

This is a place we long for, one to encourage new thought,
spontaneity, spirit, elders in any form.

The place will be different in each person.
We get to a point where intelligent companionship,
a lively, walking group, feels necessary.

## Inbetween Deaths

I do not want the last thing I say to anyone
to be how I feel something has gone cold in me
and I don't love you as much as I used to.
You always want the truth, don't you?
Well that's how it is with me at the moment.
I don't want that to be the last thing someone
like you hears from me, and the way to make
sure that does not happen is not to indulge
any moments of mean, prideful self-critique,
these failures of the heart to keep time in
the dance we are set down in the middle of
every day. Do not say it. Refrain, because
just one small step-minute more and it will not
remain true. It never stays long in that cold place,
the heart, or if it has in your experience, don't dwell
on those examples. My father's last words to me
were *Drive carefully. I can't afford to lose*
*anyone else.* Mother had died some weeks earlier.
Born in 1899, he was seventy-one in 1971.
Mother had died on May 5 that year,
of lung cancer. He was about to die on July 3,
of a massive stroke and heart attack simultaneously,
as he leaned to kiss the icewater plume
of the lobby water fountain. He was the head
of an old folks home standing there talking to the nurse,
dead before he hit the floor, surviving mom by
eight weeks and three days. I am seventy-one now
and living through the May 5 to July 3 segment,
the time that was such a triumph for my father's
surrendered heart. He would go out and walk
around, finding strangers to talk to. He had
unlimited attention and helpfulness for everyone.
It was beautiful to see that opening in him,

and surely it must have felt beautiful to be it.
I am not my father. In the last two days I have
turned down two invitations to talk to large
internet and magazine audiences. In his last
fifty-nine days my dad would not have *declined*
anything. He went to church every time it was
open. They always asked him to begin whatever
meeting it was with a prayer. He would just talk
with his eyes closed. Nobody had ever heard
anything quite like how he prayed those last
eight weeks, so hugely grateful he was for
the moments and the people the moments
brought to him. My refusals come because
I don't feel very freshly intelligent about
the subjects of Rumi and Islam and my own
kind of mysticism. I feel talked-out on
these matters, that I would be repeating
what I have said and written elsewhere.
I don't know that for sure. New memories
might come forward. I am lazy with
the talking-chances. In the inbetween
deaths my dad just so obviously trusted
completely that there was enough of whatever
was needed to carry him through whatever
the days made possible, and it happened that
way so magnificently. He might have said it
was the Holy Spirit, but I never heard him say
a thing like that. I must think I am such
a big deal that these chances will come around
in other forms soon enough. They well might
not. My part in the Rumi phenomenon is slowing.
I still love repainting the high desert caravanserai
retreat cells of his poems, though sometimes
I would rather be writing *this* wandering, which
I claim has its own variety of kindness and

sudden-looking-in. It is a way my dad did not
have much interest in, or talent for. But I do
claim too, to be open to listening to other people's
difficulties, dilemmas, delusions, and delights,
though I don't go out hunting them as he did.
I more enjoy scooting about like a zigzag
waterbug above the motionless Chinese goldfish
hung in the living jade of a shadow from where
one of them may, one will, suddenly twitch
and gobble me out of this talking any second.

## The Splinter and the Riversticks

I get a splinter on the outside right
of my heel. I need help. I call Benjamin.
He says, Come on over. I take a papersack
of implements: needle, tweezers, mirror, flashlight.
Tuck is hiding in the middle of the floor
under a thrown-off pile of blankets.
Are you ready to help?

I prop my leg high on a chairback.
Surgeon Benjamin. It's in sideways.
Tuck close in over his shoulder
like a second head holding the flashlight.
It's like finding a feather of hay
in a needlestack. You are too clever
for your own good, Tuck. I think I've got
part of it. These tweezers are so rusty.
They were in the back of the medicine cabinet.
Last time they were used was on my foot
forty years ago. This is blood poisoning central.
Rilke died from a thorn-prick. Poets ought
to die from roses. But that's a myth.
Rilke died of leukemia at fifty-one.

I'll tell you a noble death.
I went to Sunny Pressly's funeral.
Big overflow crowd. The preacher said
Sunny didn't come to church much,
but in hot summer he would quietly
back his pickup to the church steps
during the service and put big slices
of watermelon there, so that when
they came out from church, they'd each have
a big cold sweet piece of watermelon.

Is that not true communion?
He would string them out down
the dinner-on-the-grounds counter too.
Kids loved him to pieces.

Let's leave the remnant in,
not good to dig too deep. Remember Achilles?
His one vulnerability was where his mother held him
when she dipped him in the River Styx.
She forgot she needed to douse him twice
to get the job done, holding him by the other heel.
So he had that one place where he could be hurt,
or killed, like me. My mother held me by the throat.
That's why I stammered, like Billy Budd.
I still have episodes of rage and jealousy
and disengaged passive aggression.
Otherwise, I am perfect and impervious.

Superman has kryptonite. Right.
That was so disturbing when Superman
went limp and flightless, a barely even
ordinary man. I know what riversticks are.
What? Ones that float by in a race. A logjam.
That was a riverstick I had in my foot.
If it were big enough, I could walk on water.
Or run. You could take off running. I'd be
strolling the side of a big moving hill
of ocean. Here comes the top of it
under me—now I'm on the other side.

## The Scar on the Back of My Right Hand

I have an inch-long scar
on the back of my right hand.

It has been there sixty-eight years,
since I was five.

I did it to myself,
but I was goaded into violence
by parental punishment.

I don't remember what the infraction was,
something to do with the refrigerator.

Maybe just standing there with the door open,
looking in for too long, letting the cold out,
that being a big deal, during WWII,
during the summer.

I was punished by being closed in my mother's bedroom,
confined there for an indeterminate time,
five minutes being eternity.

I went to the window glass and struck
toward the bluff and the river
with my five-year-old fist. The glass broke.

I do not remember what next.
Some cry of pain got me out
of that refrigerated rage.

The slant white scar, slash of light,
a saved bit of fishline, reminds me
how other held breaths tightening in my chest
need to break outloud, be let outdoors,
over the bluff edge, down into the river.

## The Tuesday before Thanksgiving

Granddaddy, can I use the Clubhouse to have a mini-pre–Thanksgiving Dinner with my friends on Tuesday night? If you promise to do some dancing. That place needs some dancing. I can promise that.

So sixteen of her friends have a potluck giving of thanks. They write me a large, decorated with multicolored sharpies, poster-sized thank-you note. I think my son Benjamin (Briny's dad) is going to look in on them. It turns out he thinks someone else will look in and be the part-time chaperone, but no one does.

They had the place to themselves however many hours that went on. It is all cleaned up perfectly when I next go in. Just one thing off-kilter. The two big nautical stripes on the navy blue comfort on the California kingsize tempur-pedic downstairs, those stripes are going north-south instead of east-west. Horizontal instead of vertical. I ask Briny. She says, Oh, we all piled up in that bed under the covers to watch tv.

Seventeen sixteen-year-olds supinely ranged along their lumberous lengths like 4x4s under the canvas at Armstrong-Dobbs. Once they do that, folks, there is hardly any going back to the dancefloor. She has no shame about telling me, nor should she. God, I love that girl. I feel like we should talk a little more, though, so I devise this Writers' Club exercise.

We meet at a table in my coffeehouse. We switch roles. She is the grandfather who has given his inner beauty salon, his odd scriptorium, to her for the evening. I am the brilliant young woman, indigo bunting bringing in the next unimaginable glory. We write pages of dialogue for thirty minutes. You are having more fun than me, Granddaddy, she says finally. I know.

I suggest she begin, Well traditionally. . . . But she's having none of that. She begins, I know you kids like to watch the racy television.

I begin, What are you afraid of, Grandfather dear? Some legal liability? You don't want your sacred space turned into an unsupervised teen sexual experimentation lab, a black hole for erotic trancing, a pollenacious pile that moves without volition? Is there a subterranean creepy-crawly in your unconscious, Grandfuddy darling, is that it?

Well shoot. This is all way beyond my experience, she answers with my mouth. We had hayrides, but that was mostly singing *Lost and Gone Forever Clementine*. We weren't allowed much touch, so it became very charged. You know, charged.

I understand. Henry James and the unlived life, the Beast in the Jungle, I say as her.

You've read that? she screams as me.

I can't make it through the first page, but my English teachers like to talk about it. Advanced Placement, don't you know. I confess, as her. But listen, Granddaddy, seriously. Pearl Harbor is next weekend, and the Clubhouse is so perfect. The junior class History Club, we want to honor the war dead by filming a kind of documentary, combination old-time swimming hole and the sunken battleship *Arizona*. You know, *Saturday Evening Post*, 1943. We can make the Clubhouse basement watertight, tape it up, flood it with the garden hose. The school has cameras with lights that work underwater. Nighttime skinnydipping, yay. The guys will play the actual sailors come back to life, floating up young and naked. They're still down there, you know, in the *Arizona*. Voiceover's already written, faculty sponsors. What do you say?

She responds immediately as me. Heck, why not. I'll be gone the next two weeks. Less I know the better. You may need some pool supplies and brushes for the cleanup. Charge them to my account. Be sure the power's off.

Walby knows all that. Where's the fusebox?

In the closet by the waterheater. Might need to be cut at the pole. Bye Sweetheart.

Way cool. Bye granddaddy. You are so awesome.

## Tuck's Coach

Tuck is seven.
He has a new baseball coach,
big guy, who makes it clear
at the first practice that the fathers
along the fence are not to yell things
to their sons, and the sons
are to keep quiet and listen
while he is talking. The punishment is,
*Take a lap. Run a lap.*

This is important stuff.
This is human life.
We are going to keep score
and give it everything we have,
not like tee ball last year,
no calling balls and strikes,
no keeping score. That was just silly.

Tuck runs up to him later,
says, *Can I run a lap?* Coach turns his face away,
*Not yet.*

## Piecemeal

In the last months of his life D. H. Lawrence
wrote what was later published as *More Pansies*,
a pun on *pensées*, French for *thoughts*,
as well as reverence for the sassy flower
with its Gauguin-colored crowd of countenances.

> *The future of religion lies in the mystery of touch.*
> *The mind is touchless, so is the will, so is spirit.*
> *First comes death, then pure aloneness, which is permanent,*
> *then the resurrection into touch.*

Touch comes back at the end
to the wonder of skin
that it was for the infant hand
on the father's forearm.

Images of distance return: *as far as a fish is*
from the moon, for instance. Fish feel
moonpull, but they cannot touch it.
Moonlight fills the tide they swim
with all-over luminosity,
but not touch, not the most wanted.

I remember reading aloud Lawrence's "Ship of Death"
to a class in 1965, teaching my first sophomore survey.
It has been forty-three years since I felt teary and noble,
looked at by twenty-year-olds now in their sixties,
if they are here at all. Some slid out the back,
drafted on to Vietnam.

What is it he urges us to build, this ship of death
to carry us each into the next?
What is the thing we must make?
What is the vehicle of soul-travel?

*Piecemeal the body dies*, when it does not succumb to war.
But Lawrence died at forty-four. He did not
have to deal with much piecemeal:
sight dims, muscular strength diminishes,
the right hand's grip on a stuck jar's lid,
libido, the phallus' stance, the spine's superb stoop
to pick up something dropped. The whole
dance-feel and slide of feet on ground.

Numb and dumb we gradually become.
Honesty about that is a glue
that holds our ship together,
timbers of touch, keel, rib-joist,
backbone, chin, mast, ankle,
shin, knee, railing, thigh.

We are twelve. It is a summer evening
swimming party, Sandra Martin and I.
Others are nowhere apparent.

By ourselves under the floating dock,
treading cool lakewater, sometimes
holding to a strand of the spiderweb
of iron rods above us that fix
together fifty-gallon drums.

To say she surprises me is not enough.
She delights, she illuminates, she reaches
wordlessly with her tanned, satin-soft, strong
thighs to hold my right thigh in her two
as tongs might close around a bright coal
to shift the fire's attention in a forge.

The moment she holds me
with her smoothest warm pliers,

with her thoughtless daring,
leaves me fearlessly afloat.

What is it Lawrence urges us to make?
Music, boatloads of music.

## Rise & Fall

Late November afternoon.
The windy flicks of red-brown light coming down
are birds sometimes that rise to a next branch.
Other flickerings, the leaves, do not.
They keep the float-down flying
of wobbly, no-longer-trying, dead-tired wings.

## November Nights

The last thirty years have brought a change to how
I work on writing. I used to like to go to a cabin
on Fightingtown Creek in Fannin County in
the north Georgia mountains. I used to work alone
for days, alternating between building a monumental
stone wall to keep the creek from eating out from under
the concrete block piers the house rests on, and letting
poems flow into shapes that often mention my adoration
of that creek's going by, and whatever it is flows around
and through us that that is metaphor for. Heraclitus
and I love to sit down up to the neck inside such music.
Company is more important now than ecstatic solitude.

At seventy-four, I have pretty much stopped stonework.
I keep thinking I am going back to it, but I don't act
on the thought. Almost every night now I walk
to this coffeehouse full of college students studying
and talking. Music playing. Johnny Cash tonight.
Lucinda. The students sing along with it so unself-
consciously. Uncivilized, almost primal. Oh, I used
to want a high-walled garden. Now I prefer a corner
in the open courtyard of a caravanserai well-used
by sugar merchants. Sometimes I sit up late-late
watching old movies and go to sleep in my chair.
I wake in sunlight at seven and go upstairs for proper
sleep in a bed, with my elaborate pillow arrangement.
I do so love these November nights that begin early
and last long—enormous, enveloping darks.
I have never considered suicide. Nothing is petty
or trivial, not really. It is a failure in my life that
I do not allot time to listen to classical music.
Mahler, Handel, Mozart, Beethoven. These would
maybe loosen new spontaneities in me, conversation
being the thing now, a kind of music to live inside.

Here you must hear now the opening of Mahler's
Ninth Symphony. The slight, small sounds that seem
to be waiting and walking with us in an *andante
comodo*, the convenient ambling along that is
a slowing and starting up as something catches
interest for a moment in one or the other of us,
like music heard inside watersound, as I once did
by that creek in the cabin with such uncertain
foundations, a building chorale, Beethovenish, but
with even more majesty. It was so real that I walked
outside and started down the creekside path—it was
night—oddly imagining the Stuttgart Symphony
and Chorus might, most improbably, be camped
on the property next door. I soon turned back to sit
in the dark and fully hear the music that was rising
from within, as the practice of joy in my soul.

## A Perfect New Moon

Over the house next door, as I walk out,
just where the sun set earlier,
is a new moon supremely level
like a thinnest jewel gondola
with the circular sail fitted over itself,
prow to stern, that first made us want
to make something new, to say or sing
a reminder that we have this inside us,
this sailing membrane-embrace,
so now we can be and love
its beauty and never fail to.
We may be sure of something.

## Working Parts

The tiniest grasshopper is on this desk tonight. I keep thinking I must have killed him (or her) inadvertently, because I do not see where he hop-flies off to. It is like he jumps into invisibility, then lights here again on the back of my hand or on the paper, this creature no longer than three ballpoint pen dotmarks (bold), no wider than one, yet with perfect green wings and eyes, brain, knees, thyroid, memory, enthusiasm, balance, and courage. I may really have smushed him now. He has not shown back from that last trip he made into and out of the finite. How many millions of years has he been part of this being alive we are? How many billions was the sun here before this jumping in and out of light began?

# Boscage

Our love of place is part
of the love we have for presence.
So while I wait for you, I write in praise
of a kind of place I am drawn to.
Call it *boscage*. Say it sustains my essence
and holds the moving pattern that I am,
this I make niches and sidedoors in,
portals into tangle and enmeshment.
Boscage is where trees and vines and shrubs
and middlesize groundcover grow
so tightly woven together,
you must work in the edge
with small handshears clipping
and pulling out what you have clipped
to make a rounded cubicle
for a Yoshino cherry or crape myrtle
that you have brought from the nursery.
Ancient Taoist texts say that the first rulers,
the Three August Ones, had no rules,
yet people followed them. As gradually
over centuries presence became less real,
less rooted, regulations became more necessary,
and in the artificiality of that,
there was less honoring of boscage.
It survives now mostly along highways
around and *within* odd houses that persist
between car-fixing businesses.
Boscage, a thick stationary summerstorm
of nothing-becoming-nothing-more
than more-nothing, mist and xylem,
water and thread, and medicine for me.
House of hedge crisscross, I sleep within
a wedge of boscage, wiry haven of nightsingers,

shadow-happy snakes, wary chipmunks,
cramped and twisted sluice-ducts
pouring green in and emptying out
aerosols to the windy sun. Boscage be
my scutcheon and song. Boscage
be my scuppernong wine, viny insideout,
bowered tump of grasses, webbed-cave
sleeping eyrie, scrubduff haunt-patch,
complete darkness for when you
will be inside this with me.

## Iron-Knocking

You can love, and you do love,
the iron-knocking sound of a train going past.
You are close to it, the iron-against-iron dull knock.
You do not know what is making it.
It is not rhythmic. A random
clondam iron      dome-conk      whuhh
calling you to slow waking in darkness.

      mondam iron-wunk

## Catkins

April 8 out my upstairs window.
The white oak is reaching miniature hands toward me,
toward everyone, a big sphere of little hands,
each holding a sprig of seaweed
from the earth-ocean they rise, faceless, out of.
Catkins be their name.

They are not seeds. Acorns are the seeds
of these strong-standing, reach-down-deep elders.
The catkin parsley they hold
has some other purpose for their continuing.
This foam of exuberance, extrabubbly in the greenery,
are male flowers of hopeless innumerability,
clumps of alphabet on the ground.

Catkins are strands of pollen.
The females they are looking for are microscopic,
high up and pollinated by the wind.

Why some language is so beautiful it makes us cry
we do not know, just that we want to hear it again.

Catkin beget acorn beget oak. It is true.

Catkin begat acorn begat oak.

But sometimes the sequence is broken—
too much rain, too damp for too long,
so there are very few acorns in the fall
and even fewer oak trees
beginning to grow next spring.

There is a waiting we can learn from trees,
something deeper than patience. They keep
our soul's perfume in the resin and in the grain

of their spelling, in their spilling this scattered
expensiveness. Let me stay in love
with such becoming, the sounds we hear and make,
as we cry out to give the night
something kin to catkins,
or maybe more like peepers
that come singing out of low places
in late March, their notes and alphabet,
peepers and catkins in syncopation,
to remind us how another round
will come that never was.

## Darling

I am beautiful. Do you love me?
You may kiss my neck if you want to.
How could you not want to?
But remember, I am tricky,
most impossible to follow,
and will not be here much longer.
While you have the chance then
to talk and be inside my presence,
you should try to be more aware
how quickly all this slides away
and so act with some dispatch.
Live deep within your own beauty
as you repeat after me, I am beautiful.
Do you love me? The poem at this point,
you know, might loop into itself
and start again, like Pete and RePete
sitting on a fence, but no. Nobody falls off.
It goes instead: *I am beautiful.*
*Do you love me? Of course, you do.*
*I love you too. Let's take a walk.*

## Celery Hearts

Sometimes I take a plastic baggie
of finely chopped hearts of celery
into Scholtzky's sandwich shop
concealed in my bookbag and empty it into
their bowl of chicken soup with rice,
just what it needs for taste and crunch.

It is eccentric to chop and bag and carry
surreptitious vegetables into restaurants,
so I shall keep doing it,
because I like every part of the process
and because maybe it gives a little shock
to the cultural conditioning of those at nearby tables.
You cannot go wrong doing that work.
Think how great it will go into the steaming wonton.

Additions to consider. Chopped garlic clove, yes,
and several turns of the peppercorn grinder
into the baggie's mouth before sealing.

Now shake gently sideways
your fancy evening handbag of light green.

## Two Squirrel Stories

An old friend stands by Rinzai's bed as he is dying.
Have you forgotten?
Zen masters usually have something to say at the end.

Rinzai points to the ceiling. *Listen.*
Squirrels running across the roof, bickering.
He smiles. He dies.

He lets *Listen* be his last word,
along with the sounds the squirrels make
bumbling so beautifully.

That was eleven hundred years ago.
Now, last week, Michael Bailey on a ladder
reaches to clean off the sticks and leaves
from the top of a secondfloor airconditioner.

There is a long-dead alarm horn up there too,
that a former owner thought would scare off burglars.
Wonder what was set to trigger it?
It does not warn Michael Bailey.

A squirrel bites his finger, jumps up to the roof peak
and off . . . circles twice in the air,
down around an axis of himself like a treble clef,

lands flat as a note, and lies there,
full out on his wingspan in the leaves,
a Chinese character for *flying squirrel.*

> *That was not me that just did that.*
> *I am brown. What you saw overhead*
> *was creamy white.*

Did he break the skin?
It was not that kind of bite.

Michael Bailey himself has no business being alive.
Twelve years old, I saw him jump from a waterfall ledge
near Boone, a hundred feet at least.

Forty-two now, less jumpy, racing dirtbikes.
I sent him that video that emailed around
of those Norwegians in wingsuits
skirting the fjord's rockface
and just missing the highway hairpin turn.

Michael Bailey's love of ecstatic flight
has so pushed his fear genes into subordination
they do not mind following behind silently,
with a state-of-the-art camera, just out of arm's reach—
rather than screaming as they should be.

## There Ain't Nothing Like It

You know that guy last night
talking about he's from Beaumont, Texas?

He's broke down out here in the parking lot.
He could do worse.

Did Carol bump her head
out there or something?

Stay out of those woods.
They give you trouble every time.

I could waller in that stuff,
and it not bother me. Coffee?

The next thing I drink
is going to have alcohol in it, a lot of it.

Give it me for my next birthday.
I've quit counting.

Tomorrow I'll be thirty-nine for the thirty-ninth time.
Told that to Calvin, he had to get out his calculator.

Seventy-eight, idn't it? Seventy-nine.

&equiv;

In Union Springs, Alabama, at the Dollar General.
White lady doing the register
says to the black man customer in front of me,
Fish gone fishin.
Guy says, I caught a five-pound bream.

I say, a five-pound bream?
*One* pound. If I caught a five-pound bream,

I wouldn't be here. I'd be on
*Good Morning America.*

Did I hear you say, Fish gone fishin?
That's my husband. His name is Fish.

What does he like to do most?

Pause. Then she and the black man
say together, HUNT!

The man goes. She turns to me,
That's my neighbor.

We have rounded a sweet corner.
I do believe we have.

&#8773;

Something surely misheard
in a doctor's office.
A parting pleasantry.

OK. You live that nightmare,
and I'll get right back to you.
He leaves.

In a few minutes an old-old woman with a walker
comes out slow-so-slow from the examination rooms.
She sits. Her attendant follows.

I want a wheelchair.
Honey, the doctor, she says
she doesn't want you to have a wheelchair.
Looks down at the floor. I need a wheelchair.
I have to do what the doctor tells me to.
That's what she said.

&#8773;

I am standing in the radio station door, WPVM.
An older woman, about my age, gets down off the bus.

They say it's going to snow fourteen inches
by tomorrow morning. I hope not.
I've got to fly out at 11:40 a.m.

They don't always get it right.
She walks in the automatic doors next door.

She comes back out. Could you come in here
and identify an insect crawling up the wall?

Well, I've got to keep this door propped open.
Oh. I didn't know.

I leave my suitcase holding the door and go look.
It is a very tiny mosquito.
I come back out. The doors close.

The black man sitting on a bench
facing the street looks at me.
What was it? A mosquito.
She's crazy as a bat.

As if by magic the doors open again,
and she's back. Did I hear somebody say,
*Crazy as a bat?*

That was me. Don't worry about it.
Well, you best be talking about yourself.
You are right about that.

Somebody could get themselves smacked
for saying such a thing.

The conversation stops.
Me and the guy look away.

My ride comes with merciful immediacy.
We load bags to the middle seat
and never look around at her.

I should have stepped back
within her smacking range.

I should have said I'm sorry.
I'm an idiot. I hate those stupid cheapshots
as much as you do.

I did not mean to hurt your feelings.
I did not mean for you to hear.

But I do not have the courage or the presence.

I have hurt so many.
Too old to be adding to that number,
but I do, almost daily.

Is that too humble pie,
pity-poor-me? OK, next time
I'll say, I deserve it—fire away.

Then catch her hand
if she tries to hit me. Shake it.

I am not going to let anyone
hit my face, if I can help it.
That's where my eyes are.

≡

Briny is looking through a ragged tan notebook,
My friend Chris has written this short dialogue
of God with humanity, or a small group of us.

God is speaking. *Couldn't you just try*
*to be happy? You cannot imagine*
*how much vitality it took to make those redwoods.*

*And the immortals that walk among you, unrecognized,*
*unbelievable drain there. Enjoy what you got, please.*

Sounds like God wants to conserve energy.

Yeah, he's winding down.

≈

A man sitting on the edge of an open coffee place
where it blends into a parking lot, Santa Cruz.
He is talking to himself and God.

   *You, Humongous Fungus, You.*

≈

I walk into a Saturday morning breakfast place
in Copperhill. Three guys at a table.
One of them says, low but clear,

   *Give him a haircut to go.*

≈

Exiting up the slant, being helped by the stewardess,
an old man about eighty-five.
Where's that plane going now?
You have to get off here.
That's going to Wilmington, North Carolina.
I have friends there. That's a nice town.
Is your son coming to meet you?
Yes, I see him.

His shuffle quickens and his arms rise.
He loves his son so, who does not move toward him,
who stands, interrupted from his business day,
where he is by the post.
His father drops his arms, containing his emotion now.
The fifty-five-year-old dark-haired man
reaches to take his father's hand,
shakes it and smiles, and looks away.
The old man brightens. He'll take anything.
It is wonderful enough just wherever this is.

≡

A big group in a conference room in a hotel.
Them and their wives completely casually dressed.
Tee shirts and bermuda shorts, no socks, tennis shoes.

Very at ease with each other, laughing,
telling stories, all of them about mid-sixties.

No agenda apparently.
A guy walks by near where I'm sitting.
What is this hilarious group?

Bravo Company, Vietnam.

He said, Benjamin my son said,
Show me the places you have loved,
so I will know them like you have.

I will have to do that someday,
he said, when you are gone.

The small things and places
you have not told anyone of,
show me those.

I want your life
inside my life.

## Salinger in Arabic

Is it an inflammatory thing
to say that war is immoral? It is.

I mean no judgment on any young person
in the armed services anywhere.

I mean for me now at my age.
I have no business putting explosive devices
near the beautiful awareness of another human being,
much less a JDAM rocket-powered grenade
into the sleeping area of an Iraqi corporal
who is up late reading Salinger in Arabic.
Sitting up late reading with other people
asleep around you is a sacred coziness,
whether the weather be full orchestral summer,
or winter rain, wind, the anything-surround
for the changing beauty of reading.

Soldiers read totally unpredictable matter,
and I *did do the killing*, as much as anyone,
maybe more, because I often
have a microphone given to me now,
and I could have said into the amplified air
the immorality of not saying anything,
when I had the chance.

Way too many died in Vietnam (2 ½ million?)
because we so delayed our speaking.
*An ox was on my tongue*, as the watchman says
of his hesitation in the *Agamemnon*. It has been
my problem, the holding back from saying
what I feel so strongly as I walk the length
of the E concourse in the Atlanta airport
wanting to yell, *Don't go!* That's the one

the desert camouflage flies out from,
the kids with laptops.

No one else must die for a government's insanity.
Let the young man finish his Salinger
and sleep well into morning.

Though it will have to be some other late lamp
that stays on, now that one has gone out.

We were in Vietnam so long
because of a domino metaphor,
a policy we could not give up
the idea of.

Now in Afghanistan for longer,
because 9/11 anger keeps telescoping
inside its two towers.

Good and gentle Islamic souls
need to dissuade the purists among them
from violence against the innocent.
The same with us.
The pure and the impure need
to be flexible and kind
and have melting eyes like Bawa.

*Muhaiyaddeen* means
*Light has returned.*

That light, whatever you choose to call it,
is what makes being alive such a hoot
and so holy that we devise myth
and song and perfect tiny drawings of people
parading around the bulbous globe of a gourd.

That light within light
is why we love to talk and read,
and sing, and play music.

60 percent of our tax money goes to the military.
4 percent for education.

We are so slow to wake,
but surely there is time for clarity on this,
or shall we say, It is too late, and not try
to change the impulse toward war
and what it is in us that feeds it?

By small increments, I am hoping, we can begin
to dismantle this unconsciousness,
or if not, maybe the weird comedy
of our failing will keep us close enough
so that more bits of stories will be heard
about what appears in the great world
because of the money we spend
without objecting to how it is spent.

## Peter O'Callahan's Dream of Me Not Being Here

I sometimes act like I have a daring new voice
that can say anything, and maybe I do.
Maybe everyone does. I act like sometimes too
that I have touched the emptiness
Ramana Maharshi lived within and spoke of.
Or maybe it is true that I am living inside that
just as he did. But he does not seem to doubt
the region of consciousness he inhabits, whereas I do.
I think I do. Is my joy the same as Rumi's?
I will let someone else decide. My great hypocrisy
is that I have a love that I hold back
from giving away. But that's not true either.
I am just testing out sentences. Whatever
is true about how I love or don't love, am
or am not in the core of my awareness,
let all that be exposed here to the air,
opened out like blankets on the grass
in the sun. I want to be through judging
myself. I'll just be in here living and loving
without thinking so much about it, or
what you might call it. What I am more
interested in, at this moment, is something
that happened seventeen years ago.

We are at a conference in Vermont sitting up
late talking, my friend Andrew and I.
I am leaving the next morning. He is staying
a couple more days. I give him a bunch
of colorful Rumi paperbacks to give away.
Dark blue, green, red, yellow, light blue.
It is not so much generosity as my wanting
to lighten my carry-home load. Next morning
when I get up, Andrew has already gone over

to breakfast with the books. I sit on the steps
of the cabin waiting for my ride. Peter O'Callahan
is going to take me to the Montpelier airport.
He lives a mile down from the conference center
in an old farmhouse. He drives up. I get in.
He starts off saying I had a dream of you last
night, but you weren't in it. Andrew is spreading
multicolored books in a semicircle on a table.
Wait a minute. I give him my 800 number.
Please call this and leave a message about what
you see when you come back from the airport
and walk into the cafeteria. He does and says
that the books were arranged on the entrance hall
table just as he has seen them in the dream.
Now. I know that I am telling the truth,
and I would bet that Peter O'Callahan is too.
What does this mean about how we describe
the dream state and the waking state? Peter
O'Callahan asleep in the farmhouse down the road,
in effect, overhears what Andrew and I are saying,
the spontaneous giveaway of books, then goes
ahead in time and gets a visual of how a table
will look as he comes in the screen door
in the morning light as it will become. Andrew
and I have been close friends for thirty-four years.
That friendship, I suspect, is involved in whatever
transpired. Such closeness helps telepathy
and precognition. It cannot be doubted anymore
that those abilities are part of being human.
Neither Andrew nor I remember any dreams
from that night. Maybe such open-air blankness
is also part of it, and the sudden spontaneity
of the gift. Emptiness, friendship, spontaneity,
and the dissolving of the ego through public
humiliation, all that goes in the mix here.

My mentor and friend Robert has told me
and the crowd that I am drinking too much.
If you want to be a slob, go do it somewhere else.
A lot of people here are in twelve-step programs.
He is absolutely right, and I have corrected
that behavior, somewhat, mostly, trying to,
still. Ego blocks the inward building that soul
is about. When ego dissolves, it may be that
we are allowed glimpses into the connecting
nodes that arrange, align, and combine dream
states with exterior events, spontaneous moments
with the care of craft. That interpenetrating
aliveness we have no name for is making
the beauty we so deeply crave. And that involves
a shifting, oceanic community-tribe, always
new, nearby, and always far-distant, ancient.
Andrew and I and Peter O'Callahan and Robert,
and others we do not know, are weaving
blankets of listening and conversation, and
setting them out over the grassblades, over
the duff layers, mold, wet root, and sky all hugely
helping too, so busy with whatever is so
elaborately, and so absently, coming into being
as a great space of friendship. Maybe me
not being here is you and me not being here
together, walking along, and sometime—no one
knows how soon—one, or rather both of us
will actually not be here like we are now.
Maybe then we will have a better sense how
*alive* an amplitude of emptiness truly is.

## Witness

I took some LSD once,
by myself, on a spring day in the 1980s.
After an hour or so, I decided
to walk up to the grocery store.
Bell's in Fivepoints. I forget what I bought,
but when I got to the checkout counter,
a kind of miracle happened.
The kid bagging groceries shakes out a papersack,
two authoritative whips, and I see
every lightning-shaped line of the unfolding sack
as they crisscross, merge and release,
like the *shook foil* of Hopkins' *Grandeur*.
*The world is charged with the grandeur of God.*
*It will flame out like shining from shook foil.*
I clap softly, say nothing, and leave without looking back.
People may attack me for recording this here,
with good reason, because young people have taken LSD,
then thought they could fly, and died.
Young people die for lots of reasons.
I just thought it should be noted
that most educated people my age,
a little younger than Ram Dass, have taken LSD,
and most of us feel it is somewhat important
to whatever sense of spirit we might have.
I recall James Agee mentioning cocaine
so sweetly and beside the point there at the end
of *Let Us Now Praise Famous Men.*
They have been listening silently to foxes
calling each other in the dark. Then it's over,
and the listeners begin to talk and give voice
to the sometimes painful details of their separate days,
and they feel that talking is "valuable and necessary
beyond comparison of cocaine."

Ed Hicks' ex-wife Nancy has died of Lou Gehrig's disease.
Two days before her death her neighbor,
a close friend, says that she was up all night
listening to Nancy singing in her garden.
Suzanne, Ed's daughter, says Nancy always sang
while she was working in her garden.
Some inner singing kept the neighbor awake,
outside of time, pushed forward a bit, into spirit,
or pushed back to when she was healthy
out working in spring sunlight.

It is real, that singing in the garden,
though it can only be heard inside one other head,
still real, and how we all want to approach the crossover,
inside a natural working, outdoors.
With reliable folks involved, reporting
such inward experience does give a true witness,
and a good listening, to the mystery,
the beauty we live inside that is inside us,
and has so many names, and no name.

## A Sky-Opening

Now this light,
last day of June 2010,
sun going down, gone down,
but with a glow out the east window
so strong an overall surround,
hard rainstorm just over,
pinkish blue, gold sky everywhere one glow,
reminding me again how it was in my childhood,
how it still is,
the way a change in light and air
makes you *have* to walk outside
to try to get closer to it
out in the yard or in the street
under a sky-opening through the trees.

## Middle Falls

*for Lisa Starr*

The Middle Falls of the McCloud River
off Highway 89 south of Mount Shasta
is a place and a presence all at once.

Looking straight through the dissolving fabric
of mist and waterfall ozone makes me want
to sing loud nothing-sounds. I do.

An eighty-foot-tall dead pine tree at the base
is very ready to take the hint
that waterfalls give so freely. *Die before you die.*
Take the plunge like I once did so trusting,
as a young, middleaged man,
the water's hold on my body.

Now I am watching you risk your life.
If you hit your head, I cannot get down
quick enough to where you are to save you.

You dive, like I did, trusting
it is time but not that time.
*Takes my breath it's so cold, you say.*
*That's never happened, you say.*

Now you climb barefoot back
to where I have found a perch to write on,
pocked greystone with lots of ants.

A tiny bird lights on the green-veiled face
covered with ferns and vines, stays there
in the showering about fifteen seconds,
then off low over the roiling cold
of the falls pond. This water

turning quicksilver in the air has dug
the perfect bath for an otter-osprey-panther,
what you are in your daring desiring.
So wash, so dance.

## Occasional

Sixty-five years ago I was eight. After supper,
as I came out of the dining hall, there on the stoop
was a pile of the *Chattanooga News Free Press*
with a big black block headline, **ATOM BOMB**.

Who would have guessed we would go another
sixty-five years and explode only one other such bomb
in an act of war? And that only three days later
over Nagasaki, very arguably a war crime.

Broadus Smith, who lived so near and so alone,
saved stacks and stacks of *Time* magazines.
They were all over his one-room apartment
and down the little hallway attached.
What was the cover of *Time* for that week,
I wonder, of our two atomic bombs?

I never knew anyone else named Broadus.
He later married Miss Mary Martin, the dietitian.
They didn't seem very happy, or very unhappy.
They probably shouldn't have married but stayed
mostly in their separate cubicles two doors
away from each other. That's just me.

It is your birthday, forty-four. Your daughter Millie
woke you up with your present, that you could sleep
a little longer, and for lunch you could come to Finn's,
the restaurant where she is bussing tables,
and watch her work. She knows your values so,
and hers, her value. Millie is the bomb,
this birthing death-day so fine.

## Seagull

Sitting on the sand, cradled
in a driftwood log seat, perfect.

Beside me a yellow and black tangle of rope,
nine inches long, knotted in the sea.
I will bring it home to thee.

I call you on my cellphone.
You, on the other shore looking east,
me west, Turtle Island behind our backs.

Coots go down for twenty to forty-five seconds,
every time I have thought to time them,
stay under fishing, chasing little slick *hors d'oeuvres*.

Though I cannot swear that's what they are doing,
just what birders tell me, those saints
of outdoor looking and listening.

Headlong, low over the surface, wood ducks.

A gull flies over, does a curve around me,
lights on the beach four yards away.

Settles in like a roosting hen, neck down into breast,
breast flat on and in the sand. Good long rest.

If I move my hand to write, will she scare, he/she?
I do. Nope. Still quiet like a carcass,
except for that fabulously alive head.

Little twitch of wings.

You said when I just called it was like
I had gotten in some catnip, my rapture.

Slurp-slurp go the Alsea River estuary waves.
Here comes fog-mist in on me, always something.

He/she is my model posing for free,
naked as any jay.

Gull-cry out on the water. He/she turns that way,
away from me, first time.

Boy and girl come wading.
Gull decides it is *now*,
off over the water near the brother and sister,
then slanting toward the parking lot.

Little girl calls out, Seagull, *seagull*.

## Hummingbird Sleep

A hummingbird sleeps among the wonders.
Close to dark, he settles on a roosting limb
and lowers his body temperature
to within a few degrees of the air's own.

As the bird descends into torpor,
he assumes his heroic sleep posture,
head back, tilted beak pointing to the sky,
angling steep, Quixotic, Crimean.

This noctivation, the ornithologist word for it,
is very like what bears do through the winter.
Hummingbirds live the deep drop every night.
You can yell in his face and shake the branch.

Nothing. Gone. Where? What does he dream of?
He dreams he is the great air itself, the substance
he swims in every day, and the rising light
coming back to be his astonishing body.

# The VOICE inside WATER

First the voice dies, then I.
First the voice, then a flowing underneath is heard,
a moment-movement-lightening,
fire and current, up and to the side,
down and sidewards the other way.

Christopher Smart, an English poet
in the time between Pope and Wordsworth,
along with his imaginary nephew William Blake
(they never met), was ablaze and rampant.

Kit Smart had cyclothymia, a kind of pulsing mania
for praying in public, any time, any place,
whether wanted or not, out loud and loudly.
He did so love his sonorous voice saying,
in the close quarters of a carriage, or before a cage
of chatt'ring monkeys, or for the pleasure
of serenely blinking lions, a few mild sets
of alligator eyes, adrift and listening, or in a church
while the preacher himself is having at it,
or behind a line of drunks peeing against a high brick wall
and within its afternoon shadow, *Praise God.*
There he is, talking to the immensity, and me.

He says about his arrest, *For I blessed God*
*in St. James's Park till I routed all the company.* (89b)[1]

He was admitted to St. Luke's Hospital for the insane
on May 6, 1757, and let out a year later
with the designation *discharged uncured.*

---

[1] These numbers refer to Karina Williamson's text. It is not easy to find a full copy of what survives of this incomplete, strange, and masterful poem. Williamson's is the best: *The Poetical Works of Christopher Smart,* ed. Karina Williamson, vol. 1, *Jubilate Agno* (Oxford: Clarendon Press, 1980). The references in this poem and its notes are all to fragment B. *Ju-bilate Agno,* in Latin, means *Rejoice in the Lamb.* For almost two centuries the poem never be-

I do not now know whether this stroke[2]
is obstacle, adversity, a hardship of the head,
or a blessing—the unexpected luck
I got dressed up for, suit and tie, and went out
in my truck early on a Sunday morning to find.

Later, Christopher Smart was forced to be admitted again,
this time to a private madhouse, Mr. Potter's asylum,[3]
where he was treated well, given books and writing materials,
and allowed to sit in the garden and work on his poetry—
still, of course, bitter about being confined.

came more than Smart's handwritten-in-the-madhouse pages. He may not have intended publication. He may have written rather for his own solitary, incantatory pleasure, though surely that is a part of every poet's motive, and the antiphonal structure, the alternating Let and For line beginnings, certainly implies a performance (probably liturgical) possibility. The call-and-response echoing (infrequent, but definitely there at times) of words and images between the Let and For lines convinces me that Smart had in mind some way of putting his Jubilate out into a larger world beyond the private voice he recorded in such careful, intense script. That manuscript of thirty-two pages is preserved in the Houghton Library at Harvard, though how and where the manuscript survived from the eighteenth century is mostly a mystery. The poem was totally unknown to the public before 1939, when William Force Stead published Rejoice in the Lamb: A Song from Bedlam (Stead's title).

[2] I had a stroke on February 27, 2011. It affected my speech, with hesitation glitch-halts, what my therapist calls verbal dysfunctions: "Everyone has several of those when reading a short paragraph." Mine were more than that, though, and my voice resonance was changed too. I called off all public appearances for four months. A year and a half later now (August 2012) my speech has almost returned to normal. There are still glitches. I find I require much more sleep, ten hours. There is no tired like neurological tired. I am back out on the road doing readings with music, but some nights are better than others. I don't want to pretend that I am not damaged. I feel it in my throat and in my head, a sense of exhaustion I have never felt before. Travel is not so breezy now. Something in me is trembling, hoping there will not be a second stroke during the stress of the road. It is all very tentative, this living, and moreso now. Fear and trembling aside, I am certainly not up to Smart's LEVEL of RESONANCE, to use his vital capitals, as I once was. Wouldn't it be wonderful to have a recording of him saying (HALF-shouting) his poems? If I record this poem, I will speak the Jubilate lines at the end, as a way of honoring Kit Smart's attempt at self-healing: to roar himself whole in the asylum, sole to crown. Most likely, though, I will never bring this poem and its notes to a reading. Too long, too willful in its wandering.

[3] The reader may want to consider this poem, with its quasi-scholarly notes, as my version of Mr. Potter's asylum, where I give myself sanctuary to indulge a few private enthusiasms, while I heal in the garden, before going out to pray loudly again in PUBLIC.

Is there such a thing as a black eagle,
crow and raptor combined, a talkative soaring one?
Perhaps, the black-breasted snake eagle
of southern Africa[4] with his glowing yellow eyes:
mustard, sandstorm, umber.[5]

I am hearing a voice, or a motion, unspoken
as I write these pages. Inwards.
In words. Atom, a tom-tom
small sound that is everything, a beat.

Such a stroke
does not hurt.
You don't feel a thing.
So at the last
let translation be smooth.
Could be the next stroke is that,
any second, my second.

---

[4] This rare bird and the other unheard-of animals here can be found in ANIMAL: *The Definitive Visual Guide to the World's Wildlife*, ed. David Burnie and Don. E. Wilson (Washington, D.C.: Smithsonian Institute/DK Publishing, 2001). Scholars have located some of the books that Smart consulted while writing the *Jubilate*: Henry Cornelius Agrippa, *Three Books of Occult Philosophy* (1651); Eleazar Albin, *A Natural History of Birds*, 3 vols. (1731–38); Alexander Crudin, *A Complete Concordance to the Holy Scriptures* (1738); John Hill, *The Useful Family Herbal* (1754); and *The Ornithology of Francis Willughby* (1678).

[5] I am drawn to the eccentric color words, which need, and often defy, definition. *Umber*, a natural clay brown originally found in Umbria in central Italy; *wenge* (pronounced venga), a rich greyish brown with copper accents. The wenge is a tree that grows in central Africa, whose wood is this color; *feldgrau*, "field grey" in German, the light grey-green of the German military uniform, 1907–45; *taupe*, a brownish-green or a dark greyish brown. Its name derives from the European mole and covers a wide range of shades. There is no agreement on what color taupe is, really, and no authority to turn to, to settle the argument; *timberwolf*, a greying white; *veronica*, greyish indigo; *celadon*, a pale sea-green from the celadon pigment used in Asian pottery and described by the ancient Chinese as having a quiet elegance "beyond description" like the spirit of Zen; *virid*, a dangerously alive green; *cinnabar*, bright red, almost vermilion, from the color of a mercury oxide ore; *bole*, a reddish earth color, from clay with iron oxide in it; *glaucous*, grey-green; *cerise*, a clear cherry red; *myrtle*, the deep green of the evergreen myrtle leaves.

Some people go to sleep one night
and do not wake up. They are not alive then
in ways they have been. In others, maybe they are.

It was a tiny cell-junction, not found on the MRI,
or any kind of scan, that went awry in my brain,
that clogged place trying now to find, or make,
new neural pathways, microgroundwater
moving through the dark inside the brain's
wenge, feldgrau, taupe.

If we had a *physical* theology,
it might be like a loose-limbed lying-down
in the jewelweed that I once did
at the end of a day's walk on the Appalachian Trail.
You have to do that to feel the luxury, a peacefulness.

A physical theology might say, to be symmetrical,
that there are as many lives on this planet
as stars in the vast void, each one a lit bit.

I once saw an eagle stoop and take a seagull to the top
of a tall pine, where it did tear and eat what meat
there is on a gull in British Columbia.

On three Hawaiian islands—the big one, Maui, and Kauai—
there is a brilliant-bright vermilion bird called an Irwi.
Very rare on the other islands and nowhere else at all.
How would our dear friend, the three-noted, five-noted,
two-note cardinal feel in the presence of the Irwi?
Inside a garden of leaf layers: persimmon, timberwolf,
veronica, celadon, virid, cinnabar, bole.

And there is a biggish cat in the Andes who is seldom seen.
No one knows how few there are. Its social unit is the individual.
It lives above the tree line, over ten thousand feet.

It has a long tail with twelve horizontal ringbands, light and dark,
true elegance hunting among grey rocks for legged morsel.

Those who get to name such things call her the Andean Cat.
I call her Felicity. She loves all the many wildflowers
at that altitude. With her lovely face pushing through
the purple, champagne, glaucous, mint, not caring
a tunket,[6] cerise.

Meanwhile Azara's agouti runs around
on the other side of South America feeding by day
on seeds and fruit and other plant material,
weighing six pounds and looking a little like a rat,
but it *barks* when alarmed, as does the formidable fossa.

The fossa lives only around the outer edge of Madagascar,
a sturdy, muscular, dog-cat pitbull snarler, shorthair, brown.

Before people came, Foss specialized in hunting lemurs,
leaping lemurs. Grab a foot with your mouth and ride it down.

Now it takes pigs, poultry, any livestock
that might be near the outside of a house.

The fossa is endangered *because* it is the top carnivore,
next to us, and that annoys us. Here Foss,
with cold starlight in your eyes.
You might not call him beautiful.

During a day a Madagascan farmer might spot
several fossas at the edge of his garden,
but I shall never see these animals,

[6] "Tunket" is an exclamatory dialectical euphemism for *hell* or *damn*. The only person I ever heard use the word is Robert H. West, eminent angelologist, good friend, department chair, doubles partner, Shakespearean, and neighbor down the street from me in Athens, Georgia, who refused to ever read *Moby Dick*. He picked up the quirky expression somewhere in middle Tennessee, I reckon. I never asked.

though I can and do love what I do not see.
But not so much as that that I can.

These animals may be already gone—
the copyright on this picture book is 2001—
though some may still be in a ragged thicket,
or scooped-out burrow, looking for what's in motion,
napping long.

I have no justification for these lines
as they appear, then dissolve, to begin again.

What do we have to say of any life-form,
but WEEP? WEEP AND SAVE THEM.
And this planet that produced us all, and love,
out of its fierce and gentle breathing-flow.

Where does water come from?

Christopher Smart says[7] water comes from
the interior of precious spirit-stones. Diamond, emerald,
ruby, amethyst, the core of those being clear essence,
which comes also to us with the marrow of platinum
and copper, mica and crystal, the mineral and jewel-soul
we taste and feel around us as WATER, moisture and spirit.

I walk out in the cold spring air, in white oak winter,[8]
to hear, always near, crows somewhere close, not seen.

---

[7]WATER is not of solid constituents, but is dissolved from precious stones above. For the life remains in its dissolvent state, and that in great powers (196b, 197b). Smart loves that dissolvent state, where the rainy powers are.

[8]The country phrases throughout can be found in that magnificent brush arbor home-coming of a book A Dictionary of Smoky Mountain English, ed. Michael B. Montgomery and Joseph S. Hall (Knoxville: University of Tennessee Press, 2004). "White oak winter" is a frost in late April when the white oak begins to bloom in the Smokies. "You can plant your corn after white oak winter."

The story we are being told by water,
coming from its jewel encasement, is ESCAPE, DISSOLVE,
KEEP IN MOTION. GIVE UP YOUR QUALITIES
TO OTHERS. Emerald-drop, diamond-water.

Do not block the voluble flood,
the voice inside water, its resonance and timbre.

In a sequence about fish and New Testament characters, Smart says,
*For a man speaks HIMSELF from the crown of his head to the sole of his feet.* (228b)

And, *For a LION roars HIMSELF compleat from head to tail.* (229b)

Then, *For all these things are seen in the spirit
which makes the beauty of prayer.* (230b)

Those lines make a case for cyclothymia,
Smart's delight in blessing the roar
of the LION IN HIMSELF,
walking St. James's Park one afternoon.

No need to diagnose him, though,
as anything other than one of our own lovely ways of speaking,
fooling around with whatever next happens to appear.

Such sentences as his come as the voice of the earth itself.

*For EARTH which is an intelligence hath a voice
and a propensity to speak in all her parts.* (234b)

*For ECHO is the soul of the voice exerting itself in hollow places.* (235b)

*For ECHO is greatest in Churches and where she can assist in prayer.* (237b)

*A man cannot die upon his knees.* (269a)

*For a good voice hath its Echo with it and it is attainable
by much supplication.* (238b)

*For the VOICE is from the body and the spirit—and is a body and a spirit.* (239b)

This is beginning to be an anthology of lines I love
from Smart's *Jubilate,* those having to do with VOICE.[9]

I have known from an early age, the second grade,
how fragile my voice is, that at any moment, it may
come out hesitant, unsure of its course through a sentence.

Or it may be strong and floating and satisfying
to the ego's amplification in the throat and the jaw
and out through the wood nymph moth-mask of the face.

One night recently after midnight,
a small bird hovering close
to the light above my back door
went around my head touching the skull
with its wings, lightly but surely.

This has never happened before.
Off then to a dogwood branch four feet away, a little wren,
trying to heal my stroked brain with
feathery craniosacral hand-flutters.

Kit Smart's cat Jeoffry[10] may well have gotten him through
his time in the asylum. Christopher himself may now be some similar help
to us, with his love of all so many things: flowers, the Greek alphabet, spices,
jewels, vegetables, birds and fish, every kind of animal,
and dead people's surnames he finds in periodical obituaries.
He does have a strong sense of what is sacred. Everything.

[9] About half of these quotations from Smart are ones that Galway Kinnell loved to include in his readings in the 1970s. The other half are my own cuttings from the *Jubilate.*

[10] The only well-known lines from Smart are from the "For I will consider my Cat Jeoffry" section of *Jubilate Agno.* Those seventy-four lines have been anthologized many times. They come at the end of fragment B, ll. 695–768, pp. 87–90 in Williamson's edition.

His lines have great joy in them because of that.
He says this of how he works with language.
*For my talent is to give an impression upon words by punching,*
*that when the reader casts his eye upon 'em,*
*he takes up the image from the mould which I have made.* (404)

Punching may be a printing term, from the forging of type,
or from his own mystical crafting, the knack for giving
a raised feel to an image, an intensity to the sound.

*For [nothing] is so real as that which is spiritual.* (258b)

*For there is nothing but it may be played upon in delight.* (255b)

LET MY VOICE COME BACK, dear EARTH,
or if not mine, then lend me Kit Smart's.
I'd as lief pray with his as anyone's.[11]

There are these times when we are spared.
SPARE this bit a while LONGER.

I was riding down Milledge talking on the OnStar phone in my truck
when my voice became garbled, then clear, then
un-intelligi-hee-bull. Left on Springdale, right on Rocksprings,
left on Baxter, on to St. Mary's emergency room in time
to get the tPA, which only 2 percent of strokes arrive soon enough for.

*For the sin against the HOLY GHOST is INGRATITUDE.* (306)

I do mean to be more grateful
as I start the next propensity to speak.

What used to be effortless
now is scored with a tightening so counter

[11] Samuel Johnson was a friend of Smart's. I am paraphrasing what Boswell reports that
Johnson said of Smart's madness: "He insisted on people praying with him. I'd as lief pray
with Kit Smart as anyone else. Another charge was that he did not love clean linen; and I
have no passion for it."

to the release that is the core of the soul,
this new voice that needs to be lifted along
underneath each phrase and word, in the aqueduct
of my mind, bearing fresh sound tenta-tively
toward song, a slow, deliberate water.

*For to worship naked in the Rain is the bravest thing*
*for the refreshing and purifying of the body.* (384)

Within you is a place, a drop no bigger than a quark.[12]
It is in your heart, all around and inside too.
There is NO BOUNDARY.

I would not call my faith weak or strong.
I would not call it anything.
I feel an auroral aliveness, powers, hilarity.
That sense is strong and constant (almost) in me.
I have no name for it, and no valuation.

*For the breath in our nostrils is an electrical spirit.* (265b)

Rain and being naked in the rain heal the brain
and give quick liquid to the voice.

Quit crying. Don't be afraid.
We will not be far, just a whoop and a holler.
Tall ancestral elders come close.
Lean back into the joy of the ground.
Cornsilk, myrtle, crimson.

---

[12] Quark. Atoms are made of neutrons, protons, and electrons, which consist of quarks. Murray Gell-Mann got to designate what we call them. He loved *Finnegans Wake.* He had wanted, for some reason, to name the tiniest particle after the sound that ducks make, which he spelled *kwork.* Then he came across the tavern line in Joyce, "Three Quarks for Muster Mark," with its comic mispronunciation of quarts. Democritus, in the fifth century BC, is usually given credit for naming the atom. He is known as the Laughing Philosopher because of his lightness, a readiness to laugh at any moment. No one has ever seen any of these things.

## Got to Stop

This highlife has got to stop,
this looking up the roots of words in the dictionary,
like *lukewarm*. I'm serious.

This eating and drinking and walking around in the neighborhood.
Way up in the Himalayas there are ants, several distinct varieties,
little lines of them along the grey rocks.

How did they get there? They walked.
No. They existed. This existing has got to stop.

This assuming of an audience. This taking of medicines,
with music in the background,
"Dancing in the Moonlight,"
book open on the table again,
this time to *peregrine*.

## What I Am Sure Of

On March 13, 2012, the fifteenth anniversary is coming of the Phoenix Lights, when thousands of people in 1997 saw something in the Arizona sky just after dusk. The then-governor, Fyfe Symington, saw it too, and his subsequent behavior is very telling, but the detail I love about the evening is the Little League game being played in nearby Prescott. It had to be suspended, not played that night, put off until the next week, because of something in the sky that was distracting the kids. Those young men are now twenty-six, and their parents, who drove them home talking in the car that night, are in their mid-fifties. I know the lawn chairs that people bring to those games and the high-spirited competitive camaraderie of the parents and coaches. What did it take to call all that off? The weather was perfect. But still, fold up the furniture, gather the blankets—chilly here in early March—close up the coolers and load them in the back of the truck. There are so many things to do before the parking lot clears. Is that thing still up there? Who first saw what and did they call out or just point? If anybody was there that night, I would love to talk on the phone. What is it I am wanting to know? That there are other forms of life in the universe that are way more technologically, and maybe more compassionately, advanced than us? Yes. I know so little, and I doubt even that. I am partial to doubt. That may be what I am most sure of. Governor Fyfe Symington kept quiet for several months, until an article appeared in USA Today (July 18). Then he held a *spoof* press conference where he unveiled an alien in a Halloween costume. "You guys are much too serious about this." In 2007, on the ten-year anniversary of the sighting, he admitted he had been cowardly, afraid of the stigma of ridicule attached (in this country) to any claim of seeing a UFO. This, even though his long-time friend, mentor, and two-time chairman of his election committee, Barry Goldwater, was seriously interested in UFO sightings and critical of the government's secretive attitude. In 1997, a Phoenix city councilwoman, Frances Emma Barwood, was the only elected official to initiate a public investigation. She spoke with each of the over seven hundred witnesses who called her office, including police officers, pilots, and military personnel. All of them provided similar accounts. One reason, maybe, that so many people were outside that night looking up is that the comet Hale-Bopp was supposed to be visible. One family that saw the phenomenon just above their car, doing eighty along the highway, said it was several football fields wide and over a mile long, blocking out the stars. Noiselessly. Then it left without a murmur. Whatever it was or wasn't deserves attention. But after talking to seven hundred eyewitnesses, what is one to do? Very astonishing, highperformance objects *do* exist. The evidence shows that, and that they have been seen many times over many decades. I am not sure how to prepare for what might come next. I go from being unconcerned, uninterested really, to being fascinated again by individual accounts, and photographs. Then I tire of the whole thing. I want to see something myself. I want to meet these folks. Bring me the Prescott Little Leaguers.

## Coffeehouse Notes

I have said it several ways, how as a child, and continuing on to now, I have been drawn to the ecstatic, with being drunk with some vitality, as when writing is coming, and I don't know what it is yet. Rumi says there is a river inside us when the soul's joy starts to move. Like when it was raining hard in the fall, in the 1940s, say when I was seven years old, and I'd go out on the backporch, where the rain was loudest and there was a daybed, and lie there under the comforts, radiantly alive and expectant. That sense of how things are seems true still, that delighted hoopla in the blood. Yeats says in "Vacillation," "My body of a sudden blazed; And twenty minutes more or less, It seemed, so great my happiness, That I was blessed and could bless." He was drinking coffee "on the marble tabletop."

It is May 2, 2011. Thirty-four years ago tonight a man came to me in a dream. I cannot say completely what happened that night. Part of it was that I felt the process of dew forming throughout a loved landscape. In dream you can sometimes feel more wholly the surround, night air condensing into droplets of cold water, so subtly in silence, and the dew was love. I felt that, and that the dew-forming and the curve of the island, the bluff, the silo, were all part of me and part of a friendship with that man, who had such love for being alive in his eyes. I felt kin to him. I still do. Bawa Muhaiyaddeen. I met him in this more solid, wide-awake world a year and a half after the dream.

This stroke has changed me, mild though it was. Something different comes through my voice now, less innocently ecstatic, more openly broken. Speech therapy, easy-onset preconsciousness of problem places, all that has some part in the throat sound now. Whinny and whoop. This night in May it is raining on and off, hard, then drizzle, then stop. The coffeehouse has a high ceiling, tin roof on top of that, and the rain now is thundering down, everybody snug and full, reading, not looking up. A young man has just brought me my coffee with a serious question. Do you know anyone in town that I could talk to about my meditation practice? Some dark things have come up, and I don't want to go back. I want to go through it. Whatever the next stage is, fear, depression, lust, jealousy, greed, bitterness. I myself have never had a meditation practice, other than a steady devotion to poetry. The twenty minuteses now and then with eyes closed, going in, hardly count. They are so infrequent. I tell him to write half a page about what has come up. I'll look at it, and see if anything occurs to me to say.

## Fox

The fox is alive around here still, though Erica never saw her fox alive, road-kill from the highway near her place in the woods. From talking to people, books she found, and articles online, she managed to cure and preserve the four-foot-long hide, so beautiful to touch, a red silk water-riffle, electrical-ions coming off every hairtip. She even included what a professional taxider-mist might not have, the penis, an inch-long doll's knitting needle full of a million possible-foxes. My mother had a silver fox coat, the fox pelt lounging around her neck with its crafty head-face over her heart, quite an amazing coat before it became so terribly wrong. Late on Westlake Drive, 5:00 a.m., I have seen a ghost-grey silver fox loping the dark uphill lawn, not-touching ground. And I have faced a red fox directly, headhigh. I was standing in an empty baptismal pool out in the afternoon nowhere of Jackson County. Say these fox fragment-stories are an album of how our souls get flatout humili-ated, then worn around our mother's décolletage, then come loping back, still and always free, in flight, to look at us again, level across an old renewal place that never much worked. What are your fox stories? Praise the fox as you would praise your soul.

## Robert and Noah

Noah and Robert are out in a boat,
on some little river near Madison,
high summer, Noah just a boy.

They see a house. They need drinking water.
Robert grounds the boat. They walk up to the place.
There are four baked apples
cooling on the kitchen window ledge,
like in a fairytale, like *Huck Finn*.

Robert takes two.
They go quickly back to the boat.
They won't miss them.     (says Robert then)

*But Dad, those apples aren't ours!*     (says Noah then)

*He was teaching me to be a pirate.*     (says Noah now)

That particular house in rural Madison, Minnesota,
may never have experienced crime before or since
Robert's spontaneous apple raid.

Robert Bly tells me this incident on the phone,
May 29, 2011. Noah has been visiting
with his fiancée earlier in the day.

*They walked around the house holding hands.*

## Original Sins

We were talking about our earliest sins as children.
One says his was putting
a baby duck on a piano stool and turning it

until the duckling slid off and broke its neck.
Mine came at the age
of sexual curiosity and also involved revolving.

I would go with two girls to a tree-sheltered
unused dirt road where we
would pull our pants and underpants down

around our feet and turn slowly like little hobbled
dervishes with genitals
open to the breeze. No duckling died, but of course

we had to stop going down there. Somebody told.
Not me. This is the first
I've said. Someone else tells of a turtle sin.

He had been taken to see the giant Galapagos.
A few children got to ride it.
He didn't. When he got home with his pet-store

turtle, a little green one, he tried to sit on it,
petulantly, and smushed him flat.
His father crafted a cigar box coffin and a burial

sermon on loving one's pets. Try not to harm
the ducklings, or sit too heavy
on this Island called Turtle. Original Sin says

we are no longer in Eden but Fallen. How then
can we help each other up?
Some say pick one something. My friend Jonathan

chose our mistake of having nuclear weapons,
so that somebody insane
or mean or just dumb enough not to see the beauty

we live inside might cause irrevocable havoc.
Now after thirty years
of talking nonproliferation he has got the Middle

Powers Initiative going. Look it up. It is good
to pick one thing
and stay with it. It is also good to keep moving

from bed to dying bed in a field hospital
like Whitman did, just
helping out whoever is there in front of him.

## It Is Raining with the Sun Out

My friend James Hillman
came to me in a dream night before last.

His glowing energy was there,
but he was a figure IN the wall, a torso-psyche,
against and inside the wall, a bas-relief.
But his voice and presence were so completely THERE.

Across the room, I was more allied with a window.
As he was with his wall,
I am, my psyche is, weeping deeply,
with and as the window-wetly.

His soul is understanding toward mine.
But *toward* is wrong, because
the great thing in the dream, the central FACT of it,
was that our psyches were blending together,
as light and moisture, as heat and air and moisture and light,
as color and form and consciousness
flow together in a DAY.

That is how it is when it is raining and the sun is out.
Whenever my mother saw that, she would say,
*The devil is beating his wife,*
not a bad or violent thing, but so-alive,
how it is when it fills to the brim,
strange and definite. Roman.

It cannot be said what goes on in a dream.
This one especially, so full of the mystery of friendship.

Which cannot-cannot-cannot
be said.

So here we are left standing in the rain and the sun
with our psyches and our dreams,
our friends, and these words.

## Blessing-Bow

Here at seventy-four, I am having an idea
what I do pretty-well, what not-so-well.

I dream. I keep a journal of my dreams,
and I put images from them in trance-poems.

I do not write or think about poetry
with a very clear intelligence. I love
certain lines and passages without getting

the whole picture, like rocks thrown against
my door without knowing who's there.

I found this piece of paper on my bookshelf
dated September 2, 1976. It records a three-part
dream from that night. I recall best

what it felt like there at the end, here
thirty-five years later. I am invited to

a dinner table with Gary Snyder, his family
and friends. We sit in the blessing-bow.

He begins, but I raise my head instead,
and open my eyes, feeling a great love

coming. The air is electrical, full of spirit.
He opens his eyes and sees me reaching

my hand toward him. He takes my hand,
still saying the blessing, which is about

filling with love for the ONE, as we are,
and amen to that. Now that old dream

feels like an approach to this flawed and
difficult, opening-out time left before

death encloses us both in its whatever-
it-will-be, full-prostration blessing-bow.

# Anytime

Anytime I read Rumi's *Love Dogs*,
I must remember to say, But remember,
Rumi and I have here mentioned Khidr,
the Guide of Souls, whom the Sufis
are careful to say must not be, cannot
be, spoken of directly, so this answer
to what the soul longs for, the longing
itself, cannot be heard as truth. Truth
is still unsayable. It must be lived,
as we are all in the midst of doing.

## Midafternoon Midsummer

Midafternoon midsummer when the big paddlewheels came by
pushing barges or self-contained in an astonishingly plush
excursion boat, people waving from the railing, Tony Heywood
and I would hear them coming and exult, and run toward
the bluff, the lookout place, and get them maybe finally
to blow the big horn bu-buh buuuhhhhhhhh for no reason.
And Jim Hitt would come down from his second-floor apartment
to stand with his hands on his hips to take in the glory of
the nineteenth century going by, Mark Twain, Wordsworth, Dostoyevsky,
Stendhal, Balzac, several civil wars, and the deliciously profound
slush-slush of the wheel digging deep for push and purchase in
the stern-swing of the bending toward the foot of the mountain,
heel of the moccasin. God. I am almost back there standing
with him again. I hear the others coming up behind us.

## We Laugh Together
*for Milner Ball*

Milner came to an event I was doing.
He sat in the back. I could see his face
through several people's heads
smiling at me, big smile.

Whoever is doing the introducing
remarks about me being a kind of rascal,
or scoundrel. I forget the word used.
Milner laughs outloud agreement. I join in,

    AMEN BROTHER

This at the end of May in a dream.
Milner died, early April.

Do we know this much about spirit?
That we laugh together after death.
I feel we do. I *know* we do, says June.

Since this stroke I feel the great beauty
of quick, spontaneous conversation,
perhaps because I cannot participate
in such a thing so well now.

But could I ever? You were always *intemperate*
with your reticence. You have a hard time keeping up now?
Let's see. Turn him out in the pasture of pure speech.

I am reminded of a time in Moorestown, New Jersey,
toward dark, winter. You are going out for your run.
You ask if I want to ride a bicycle beside you? I do.

Can you keep up? Uphill or down? Level, mostly.
So there we went. You were amazing, but I won.
*Ho-Ha*. You were on a *bicycle*. Still, I did win.

I have not seen you since this stroke.
You have never heard what my stroked voice sounds like.
Conversationally, I could not give you that. This is it.
In time, but way too late for Sunday night vespers.
My vesper-whisper is, *We miss you so.*

How did you get that wrinkle in your fender?
Do you see a point of impact? No. That's what
bothers me. It must have come from *inside.*

A goat butted it. A goat with thickly padded horns,
you know what I mean? I am not sure that I do.

Is it one of those *metaphors*? Like the pasture
of pure speech? Stay with it. I'll be back around.

We don't just laugh together in this new
pouring rain night. We sleep. We go watch
a movie and walk home afterward,
but the talking is not very satisfactory. I have to
make both sides of it up. I think I do. I might
be wrong, about many things. Not everything.
The laughing is true.

Laughing is the clearest,
most intimate way we can be back
in the presence of the dead.

# The Gift of a Comeback

*for James Hillman*

Toward the end James said he could not tell
much difference between living and dying,
his collaboration with spirit so seamless.

Soul is consciousness, and that
is still here. *Coleman, my man.*

What a tall crane you were there,
standing long in open grassy water,
taking a look around,
then a fishy-language stab,
eyes brightening with the catch.

I am crunching celery sticks in the Delta Sky Lounge,
delayed by heavy snowflakes in La Guardia,
nothing sticking, replacement plane diverted to Albany.

James, we are airborne,
six hours late in this flying bourne
where everyone but me is touching a lit field
in the half-dark current fingerplay.

I have my reading light on this messy unlined
notebook where I begin with ballpoint poems,
half-recalled dreams, reminders to-do (call Briny, call Mary),
to-get (Marie-Louise *On Dreams and Death*).

I have no device that would have given me
Margot's email telling about your burial
earlier today, which I have missed.
I need to remedy that, but I do claim this
is an oldfashioned gift from your absence,
the Morris chair that could not be fixed,
the porchlight that shone every night
for thirty-five years for the courtship

goodnight kisses on my father's side
in Birmingham's old Woodlawn neighborhood.

I might not have written down these details
had I been alerted electronically in time to make my way
to the cemetery in Thompson, Connecticut.

So this tinge of trying to forgive myself,
and at the same time to glorify me
with an oldfangled gesture.

That *fang* part is a Middle English stem, *fangen*, meaning
*just caught, newly collected, deliberately found,*
fanged by the heron's quickness.

May it make a comeback, that past participle, *fanged*,
and may you too, in dream, come back, not for long,
just for another laugh. *To find*, in Arabic, did you know,
means also *to be in an ecstatic state? Wajada.*
Also, *to lose oneself and to become wealthy.*


January 28, 2006—a letter typed on an odd-shaped piece of green paper.
"Dear Man, I miss seeing your fruzzled head and small twinkly eyes. Are you
well. I'd like to hear that voice of yours, say any old thing, or something BIG
from 600 years ago. I won't be in Atlanta in June. I'm pulling back and fuss-
ing around more. I did finally read the commentary in *The Drowned Book* that
you suggested (imposed on my Jewish obligatory conscience to read) and
was overjoyed, really and truly, happy with it, from it. You've got a freedom of
phrase or rhythm or an access to a little pile of Georgia kindling wood that is
lightweight and touches off big logs burning. Lucky man. Let me know when
you get North and East. We have not danced together for ten years! James"

April 6, 2006—fax from Palermo, Central Palace Hotel stationery. "To my
great, great regret, I must abandon the project of accompanying you to your
anointment . . . (I was going to Iran with Robert Bly to get an honorary degree
from the University of Tehran.) Love to the old rascal Robert and to the sing-
ing spirits of old Persia."

August 7, 2006—a card with a picture of a wolf pup howling. "My man: I'm to do a thing on dogs—did your friend Rumi ever mention a dog in any way in all his jillions of inspirations? I am especially interested in BAD DOGS, evil, smelly, shit-eating fuckers, who kill babies and bite achilles tendons, and lead the soul to death. See you in April. How did Ralph Reed do in the Georgia primaries? Love & Kisses, James"

October 2, 2006—a Margot email. "James is now eating a pear that is a little overripe—on the edge of mealy—but it had a beautiful shape before he bit into it! Khidr can appear anywhere."

April 10, 2007—a fax about a panel he and I were to participate in, about "poetry in times like these." "We are always in times like these, when poetry seems vagabond and homeless. Cheerio."

January 8, 2010—a typed fax. (I had told him about a trip to Devon and how I keep going back to Plotinus, not knowing why.) "Indeed, the bleak moors, and English tea and good milk. After a certain age there is nothing else to read but your own writing and Plotinus. Robert Duncan told me he was only able to work on his own work, reviewing it, and rethinking it . . . that was near the end when dialysis took up so much energy. As for me, I still read this and that. I have always been a flotsam man. My big mouth has hardly any whale-straining teeth, so all the tiniest things come in, pass through, and who knows what traces remain or what protein I gain therefrom. But I am smiling . . . are you? A hug (not bearlike), James"

March 5, 2011—an email, seven days after my stroke. "Dear Coleman, lover of gaudy words and woody gourds, multi-talented plenipotentiary. The gods bring their gifts in many ways, few anticipated. May the encounters of these weeks replenish the gifts you have given us. Let's dance. (Remember, only the dancer can claim to be a Friend.) Love, James"

An undated fax. "And, as for a Professor of English, you have just been fired. The sentence, 'She's invited Robert and I (sic)' just won't do. You have been listening to too many highschool girls to get that case wrong."

## Heavy Rain in the Parking Lot

How does it arrive so evenly and sure
from such wobbly shapes as the clouds
of this overhanging night, as though
something regulates the flow from above
to this parking lot so solidly drenched
to every edge, where I sit inside
its powerful sound on the truck roof,
the resonance of my delight rising
to mix with the fall of its?

# Wittgenstein

Wittgenstein says, *I can imagine a religion*
*with no doctrines, so that nothing is spoken.*

I do not mean to imply by quoting Wittgenstein
that I have ever read one of his books,
or that I own or have ever looked into one.
Never turned one page of W. G.

I saw this quote somewhere else, where, I don't know.
I use it here like the charlatan I am, pretender
to knowledge, though now that I have admitted
the fraud, maybe I have lost my status as a true
charlatan. I am a fake charlatan, which might make me
a real double-negative something else, a slick comedian.

I should take his name out altogether. I don't even know
whether it is Vitt or Witt. I'll go with Vitt, as I keep going
back to this subject of his, how I too feel there can be
a religion with no belief and no structure, just a wondering
about what is sacred, and how to say it, and how
to acknowledge it as a community with places to gather,
and places to walk along and sit down at and have coffee,
and how to get electricity to such places without
disturbing the view of the sky, especially at sunset.

## Grief in the Tub

It would be so fine if we could start fresh,
the way we try to wake in a new year,
in the spring, in an autumn wind.

In a dream the other night my friend,
the late Milner Ball, paid me another visit,
this time with his wife June and his son Scott.
Virginia and Sarah may have been there too,
but it was crowded enough already.
We were in a confined space, and here's the thing:
we were completely naked, all of us,
without a smidge of embarrassment
or self-consciousness, or clothes, easily
bumping against each other, everything
grand and openhearted there,
in my mother's bathroom from the late 1940s,
the tub filling with warm water.

We each stepped in it and stood for a while,
then stepped out, with sometimes two or three
at once standing in the tubwater.
I love whatever it is that shows us
such a fragment of a look into an unseen world
where we actually wash our souls clean with others,
ablutions, dead and alive together, naked animals.
We were not preparing for anything.
Nothing was said, no speaking,
no sound but the water running.

NOTES

"Starting Out from Ted Hughes' Letters." *Letters of Ted Hughes*, selected and edited by Christopher Reid (New York: Farrar, Straus, and Giroux, 2007), 312–13. In a letter to his children, Frieda and Nicolas, April 26, 1971, he lists various ways for them "to earn some cash." Method 4 is "Similes—For every good simile, threepence. Make lists. We look forward to the weekend. love Dad"

Gregory of Nyssa—Martin Laird, over a number of years of wandering study, has written a book about this magnificent mystic, *Gregory of Nyssa and the Grasp of Faith* (2004). In homily 7 on Ecclesiastes Gregory says, "Having nothing it can grab, our mind slips into dizziness and confusion, and returns again to what is natural to it." In the early 1990s I was traveling in Cappadocia with my son Cole. I had wandered off by myself when I heard a voice calling me. I looked up into the sheer overhanging rock. Nothing. Then I saw Cole's smiling face from a tiny, head-shaped oval in the stone directly over me. He had climbed up a passageway hollowed out by the monks to give me my own moment of dizzy return to what was natural, my fear and my love for him. *Please get down from there.*

Plotinus (204–270 CE), Ennead, III, 8, 1—"Are we contemplating as we play? Yes, we and all who play, are doing this, or at any rate, this is what we aspire to as we play." From the A. H. Armstrong translation in the Loeb Classical Library (1966–74).

Plotinus, Ennead, III, 363—"Every action is a serious effort toward contemplation, compulsory action more than voluntary." Copied into a 1981 notebook of mine.

"My Face and My Voice." The problem about who legally owns letters is more complicated than I imply. The writer of the words owns the copyright. The one who receives the letter owns the paper (and the ink?). I edited this writer's language some. How much, I do not remember, and I have lost the actual letter. So here we are.

The September 21, 1800, Blake letter has been slightly rearranged from how it appears on p. 802 of *Blake: Complete Writings*, ed. Geoffrey Keynes (New York: Oxford University Press, 1957).

"Accordion Sections." "Clouds," by Wisława Szymborska, is from *Poems New and Collected, 1957–1997*), trans. Stanislaw Baranczak and Clare Cavanagh (New York: Harcourt Brace, 1998), p. 266. The reference to "nonspecific anniversaries" is on p. 214.

"Old Men Out Walking." The Plotinus quotes are from *The Essential Plotinus*, trans. Elmer O'Brien, S.J. (New York: Mentor Books, 1964), pp. 137–38.

"The Splinter and the Riversticks." Rilke died in 1926. A year earlier, gathering roses from his garden, he pricked his hand. The small wound took a while to heal. His arm became swollen, but that had no relation to the leukemia diagnosis. Still, the rose-death story became a persistent myth.

"There Ain't Nothing Like It." A few years back my friend Ed Hicks is at a lake cabin, doing carpentry on a Saturday morning with friends. A lake near Troy, Alabama. A young man, sixteen years old, is new to the group that day, brought there by his grandfather Joe Bob Allen. Ed likes to play with words when he's working, turn things around, say them backwards, all sorts of spontaneous mischief. While he's measuring, sawing, nailing. Finally, the young man puts a board right where it needs to go, perfect fit, and tries to get in on the verbal woodworking. But he does it awkwardly. Ed throws a little knob of leftover lumber at him. The boy then gets off a good one in response, some new variation. While everybody's laughing, his grandfather Joe

Bob leans back on the deck and says to the sky, "There ain't nothing like it." Ed does not remember what the wordplay was that Saturday, but you get the idea. There are spacious moments that break your heart. What we're given.

"Piecemeal." The "future of religion" quote is on p. 611 and "The Ship of Death" on pp. 716–20 of *The Complete Poems of D. H. Lawrence*, ed. Vivian de Sola Pinto and F. Warren Roberts (William Heinemann Ltd., 1964; rpt. New York: Viking compass edition, 1971).

"Salinger in Arabic." The startling percentages about the discrepancy between what our government spends on weaponry and what it devotes to education may be close to being true. It is very difficult, impossible maybe, to calculate the financial cost of war. Never mind the soul damage, the terrible loss of young life, those brilliant possibilities gone. We literally do not keep the books on the cost of waging war. The Congressional Research Service can tell us what was appropriated from 2001 through 2011 for Iraq and Afghanistan: 1.3 trillion dollars. But that does not include many things: the debt servicing necessary, the expenses hidden in the Pentagon's base budget, and the medical care and disability benefits for the injured, just to name three. A group of academics has put the estimate at well over four trillion. Accountants, those careful watchers, might do well to turn their attention to these matters. Representative John Lewis (D-Ga.) has introduced a bill, the Cost of War Act, which would require the Department of Defense to publish on a public website a running account of the cost of our ongoing wars. If we saw what we are doing clearly spelled out, we might think of something else to do with the resources. Good man, John Lewis.

"Occasional." The *Time* cover for August 20, 1945, is a red sun (Japan) with a rough black X across it. No words.

"Wittgenstein." The quote I reference is not something Wittgenstein wrote but something he is alleged to have said.

# ACKNOWLEDGMENTS

Some of these poems have appeared, often in slightly altered versions, in various periodicals. My gratitude to these publications and their editors for permission to reprint here.

*Five Points*: "Darling" and "Hummingbird Sleep."

*Georgia Review*: "Starting Out from Ted Hughes' *Letters*," "My Face and My Voice," "Lightning Bugs and the Pleiades," "My Segment on the *NewsHour*," "Inbetween Deaths," "November Nights," "Got to Stop," "Blessing-Bow," "The VOICE inside WATER," "Piecemeal," "Catkins," and "A Perfect New Moon."

*Smithsonian*: "Midafternoon Midsummer."

*Southern Poetry Review*: "Word Choice," "Rise & Fall," and "Heavy Rain in the Parking Lot."

*Zone 3*: "Witness."

The "In Union Springs, Alabama" section of "There Ain't Nothing Like It" appeared first in *Winter Sky: Poems 1968–2008* (Athens: University of Georgia Press, 2008).

CPSIA information can be obtained
at www.ICGtesting.com
Printed in the USA
BVHW071239090521
606888BV00009B/866